WROUGHT IRON
AND ITS DECORATIVE USE

WROUGHT-IRON BALUSTRADING OF GRAND STAIRCASE, CAROLINE PARK, MIDLOTHIAN.

WROUGHT IRON
AND ITS DECORATIVE USE
with 241 Illustrations

MAXWELL AYRTON
AND
ARNOLD SILCOCK

DOVER PUBLICATIONS, INC.
Mineola, New York

Bibliographical Note

This Dover edition, first published in 2003, is an unabridged republication of the work originally published by Country Life, Ltd., London, and Charles Scribner's Sons, New York, in 1929.

Library of Congress Cataloging-in-Publication Data

Ayrton, Maxwell.
Wrought iron and its decorative use : with 241 illustrations / Maxwell Ayrton and Arnold Silcock.—Dover ed.
p. cm.
Originally published: London : Country Life, Ltd. ; New York : Charles Scribner's Sons, 1929.
Includes bibliographical references and index.
ISBN 0-486-42326-3 (pbk.)
1. Wrought-iron—England. 2. Decoration and ornament—England. I. Silcock, Arnold, 1889– II. Title.

NK8243 .A8 2003
739.4'5—dc21

2002034892

Manufactured in the United States of America
Dover Publications, Inc., 31 East 2nd Street, Mineola, N.Y. 11501

PREFACE

When a thing is old, broken, and useless we throw it on the dust-heap, but when it is sufficiently old, sufficiently broken, and sufficiently useless we give money for it, put it into a museum, and read papers over it which people come long distances to hear. By-and-by, when the whirligig of time has brought on another revenge, the museum itself becomes a dust-heap, and remains so till after long ages it is re-discovered, and valued as belonging to a neo-rubbish age—containing, perhaps, traces of a still older paleo-rubbish civilisation. So when people are old, indigent, and in all respects incapable, we hold them in greater and greater contempt as their poverty and impotence increase, till they reach the pitch when they are actually at the point to die, whereon they become sublime. Then we place every resource our hospitals can command at their disposal, and show no stint in our consideration for them.—(Samuel Butler, *Essays on Life, Art and Science.*)

THE latter part of the above-quoted passage from Samuel Butler, although not strictly *ad rem*, would minimise the effect of the whole if it were omitted. The *Essays on Life, Art and Science* are literary masterpieces, and few men have written about art more charmingly or with greater insight than Samuel Butler.

In these pages no attempt to emulate his clean-cut grace of style has been made, but his form of critical appreciation has been followed in preference to the too common method of writing a mere catalogue of the features of interest in each example.

The personal factor has been given a prominent place. The character and special environment of the smith, his virtues and failings and his reactions to the moulding influence of experience and the fashions and economic conditions of his day have all been taken into consideration in assessing the æsthetic and practical value of his handiwork.

The invention of cast iron and its uses have been noted, but in the main this book deals with the history of wrought iron only. The development of the craft can be followed in a summary fashion merely by turning over the pages of illustrations which follow.

For these magnificent illustrations and for constant and valuable help and advice in the preparation of the book the authors wish to thank the publishers (*Country Life*) and Sir Lawrence Weaver, who gave so much assistance in the early days of preparation. Among other writers for *Country Life* we desire also to confess our indebtedness to the writings of Mr. H. Avray Tipping. To Mr. Starkie Gardner, too, acknowledgments must be made for the guidance given by his books on this subject. *English Ironwork of the Seventeenth and Eighteenth Centuries*, although it appeared after the Introduction and Chapters I and II of this work had been written, nevertheless proved an excellent book of reference.

We have already voiced our gratitude for the fine photographic illustrations, but we must not forget to ask acceptance of our thanks also from the large number of both clergy and laity who have allowed photographs or measurements to be taken or drawings made of examples in their charge. To those, also, who have either made drawings themselves, thrown open to us their archives, or allowed the use of their blocks, photographs or documents we wish to offer our very sincere thanks and to say that, although the list of names is too long to give in detail here, this omission does not signify any lack of full appreciation of their help. They include Mr. W. M. Myddelton, Mr. W. Beswick, Mr. F. W. Knight, Mr. G. A. Cope, Mr. L. L. Kropf and Mr. Noel Kropf.

The authors of the following books must be specially mentioned: Dening, *The Eighteenth Century Architecture of Bristol*; Friend, *Iron in Antiquity*; Percy, *Metallurgy*; Sir St. John Hope, *Windsor Castle*; Salzman, *Mediæval English Industries*.

In the case of Mr. Dening, the authors wish to make a particular note of their thanks not only for permission to draw upon material in his work, but also for his personal interest and help.

Finally, it must be said that, while this book does not pretend to be infallible or exhaustive, it does hope to arouse interest and fill a definite gap in the bibliography of wrought ironwork.

MAXWELL AYRTON,
7, *Grosvenor Street, W.*

ARNOLD SILCOCK,
97, *Jermyn Street, S.W.*

May, 1929.

CONTENTS

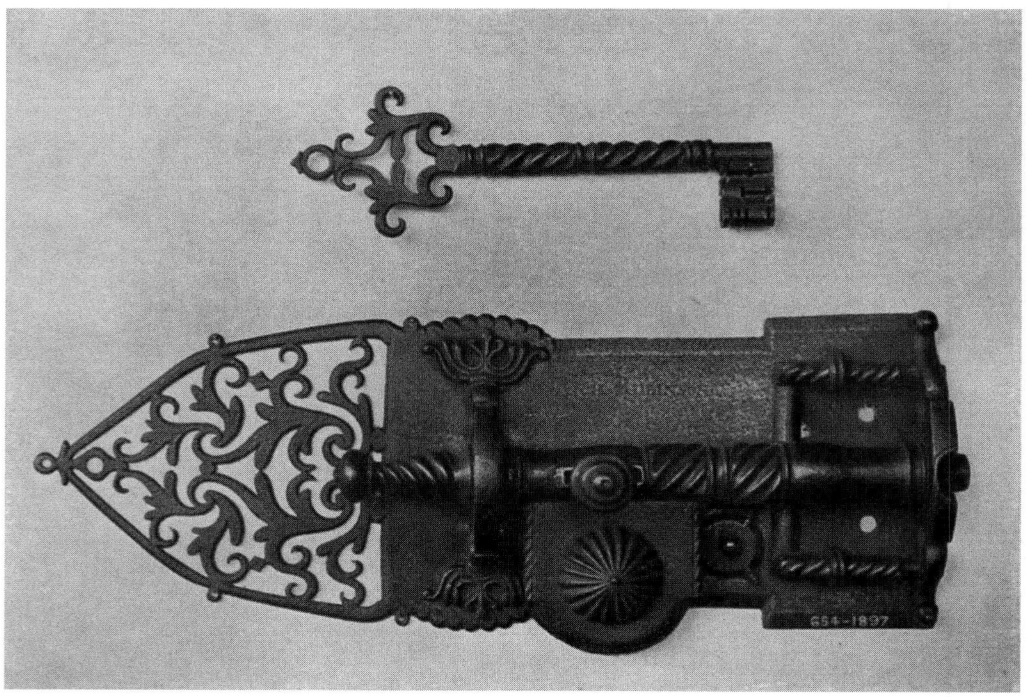
654-1897

CHAPTER I

GENERAL HISTORY

IN a work of this kind, dealing with the development of architectural iron, it is neither necessary nor desirable to deal very fully with the geological, metallurgical and technological aspects of the subject. It is, however, here attempted to give, in as few words as possible, a condensed account of the nature of iron, its distribution, early methods of manufacture and uses.

Iron is found in so many different forms and in geological formations of so many vastly differing ages, that it may be said to be the most universally available as well as the most useful of all the metals. Iron ore may be of the carboniferous period, and is then found interbedded with the seams of the very coal with which it may ultimately be smelted; or it may be found on the still beds of lakes, where it is even to-day being deposited. In some districts it is embedded in the rock, in others it is discovered lying at the bottom of peat bogs. It is universal in the largest sense, for not only does it enter into the composition of the earth's crust and of the incandescent matter beneath, but also of the meteorites flying above. The element in its pure state is rarely found in nature or in art; for the ores are composed largely of iron and oxygen, and commercial iron is derived from the ores by smelting, whereby the oxygen is driven out and carbon from the coal or charcoal takes its place. It is the proportion of carbon to iron which chiefly determines the appearance, malleability and quality of the metal: thus, in cast iron the proportion of carbon is high, in wrought iron low.

The process of manufacture has been very much the same in all ages. The ore was first crushed and then underwent a preliminary burning. The next process was to mix the calcined ore with a flux of quartz, lime or clay, after which it was smelted in open fires, for which charcoal was the only fuel used for many centuries. It is a disputed point whether prehistoric man smelted iron ores, for we have no proof at present of his having discovered the art. It has been demonstrated, however, that meteoric iron was known and valued by prehistoric man at a far earlier time than is commonly recognised.

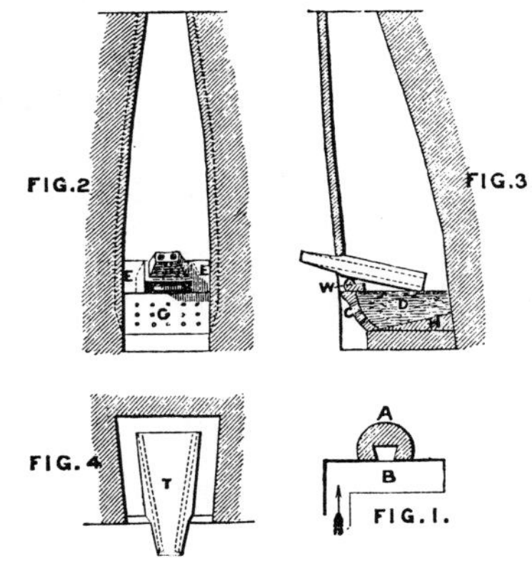

I.—DIAGRAM OF AN INDIAN FURNACE, FROM A MS. OF MAJOR FRANKLIN.
("Metallurgy," Percy.)

FIG. 1.—*Ground plan:* A, *The furnace, walls of large unburnt bricks, lined with clay;* B, *trench 3ft. deep, with sloping entrance, shown by arrow.* FIG. 2. —*Front elevation:* C, *perforated plate of clay;* E, E, *plates or tiles of burnt clay to fill space.* FIG. 3. —*Vertical section:* D, *mass of cow dung and chaff;* H, *hearth bottom of sandstone or other hard rock sloping towards front;* W, *clay wedge to regulate dip of twyer.* FIG. 4.—*The twyer,* T, *composed of two diverging earthen pipes embedded in a mass of dried clay.*

There are two bellows to a furnace fixed in front at a convenient height. Twyer is kept in place by a vertical bar, bottom of which presses on it, while top is hitched into a loop of iron between two lateral studs or staples. Height of furnace varies from 4ft. 4ins. to 8ft.; diameter at widest part from 1ft. to 3ft. 9ins. Back of furnace inclines forward. This is stated to be essential.

Not many years ago it was customary for scientists arbitrarily to divide prehistoric and historic times into definite epochs and to lay down broad divisions of these for the convenience of students. These epochs were clearly labelled and were known, for instance, as " The Stone Age," " The Bronze Age," and " The Iron Age " ; but nowadays all such rough and ready classification has gone by the board. We now know that such distinctions cannot be used to label certain periods of time, but that they merely signify that the development of a specific culture had reached a certain stage of growth. Thus it might be shown that the slowly developing civilisation of Egypt had passed through its stone and bronze ages and had arrived at its iron age at a time when the more slowly developing Britons had not progressed beyond their stone age.

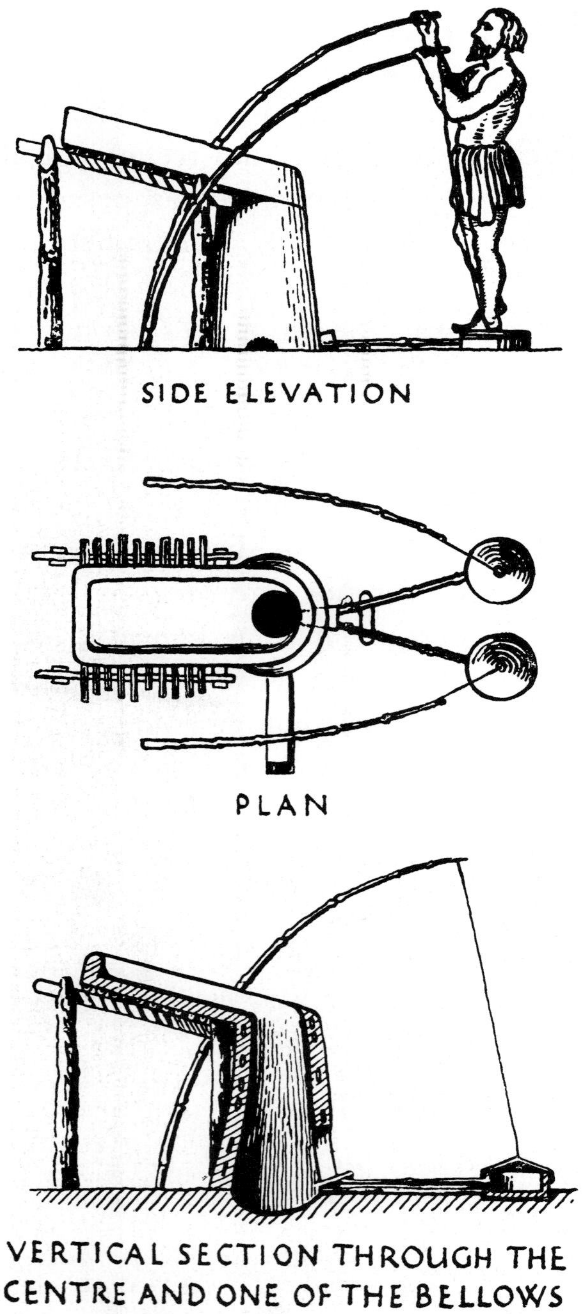

2.—INDIAN FURNACE.
(" *Metallurgy*," *Percy*.)

Proof is now forthcoming that, in various lands and at varying periods of time, Neolithic man knew many of the properties of the metal from his discoveries of, and experiments with, meteoric iron. In many cases these meteorites (sometimes of huge dimensions and many tons in weight) were known to have fallen from the skies, and were worshipped as gods ; and in one case (at Chengtu in western China) a large meteorite, protected by a temple reared above it, is still so worshipped at the present day. In some cases these objects were thought to possess miraculous properties, and pilgrims came from far and near, bringing the sick and diseased, who were supposed to find relief and healing by rubbing the affected part upon the sacred stone. In other instances the meteorite became merely the symbol of power and authority. Such may have been the thunderbolt of Zeus. In North and South America large meteorites have been discovered bearing unmistakable signs that protuberances had been cut off in the eagerness of primitive man to possess this, to him, the most precious of metals. The extent of the use of iron, therefore, may be taken to be an indication of the standard of culture attained by any given people.

The Chinese were among the first to make extensive use of iron : at all events, they had levied taxes on the metal as early as 700 B.C. or thereabouts. They had brought the craft to a high pitch of perfection at a time when the Mediterranean cultures were still in an age of bronze, and when iron was there regarded as an object of great value and interest. Too much reliance must not be placed on the early Chinese histories, but it is quite possible that records of a tribute-list, itemising hard and soft iron and approximately dated 2,000 B.C., may be authentic.

In the year 77 A.D., Pliny wrote, in his *Natural History* : " But of all the different kinds of iron, the palm of excellence is awarded to that which is made by the Seres." (" The Seres " was the name given by the Romans to the Chinese.) Thus, we find that, more than two hundred years after trade relations had been established between China and Rome Chinese iron was still not equalled by the Roman.

Of all the iron-workers of China, perhaps the most skilled are the mountain tribes living on the borders of China and Tibet. These tribes are supposed to be descendants of the remnant of the aboriginal inhabitants of China. At one time spreading from the coast to Tibet, they have gradually been driven into the western mountain ranges as the power of the conquering hordes and their dominion expanded. In fact, one authority, Terrien de Lacouperie (whose arresting theories are now somewhat discredited), has stated that prior to 3,000 B.C. these oncoming waves of invaders from western Asia first learnt of the process of iron-smelting from the mountain tribes which they conquered on their way through the Tibetan range into China proper. This theory of the Western origin

3.—THE IRON PILLAR OF DELHI.
(By permission of Sir Robert Hatfield, Bt.)

of the Chinese has again been put forward recently by Professor Ball, who has published a lexicon of Chinese and Sumerian. It is not exactly known at what date the huge iron beams (which mark the required depth to which the channel must annually be dredged) were fixed to the rocky bed of the Min river at the source of the wonderful irrigation system of western China, but this great engineering feat was probably undertaken about 150 B.C.

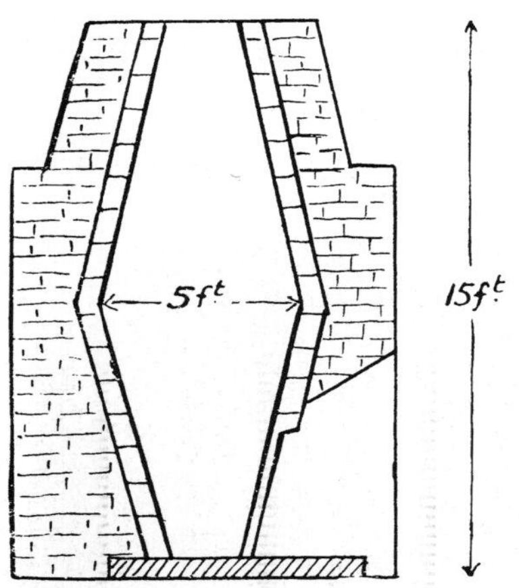

4.—THE STÜCKOFEN.
("*Iron in Antiquity*," *Friend*.)

In India, the science of iron smelting has been known for a longer period than in any other country except, possibly, in China and Egypt, for the Aryan colonists—who, about 1500 B.C., introduced their own methods of production, are said to have found an indigenous iron industry already well established. The Hindus invented, for smelting the ore, a furnace which was still in use when Dr. Percy wrote his description, and which bears a certain resemblance to that in common use all over England not many centuries ago, when charcoal was the only fuel yet discovered capable of producing a metal of fine quality.

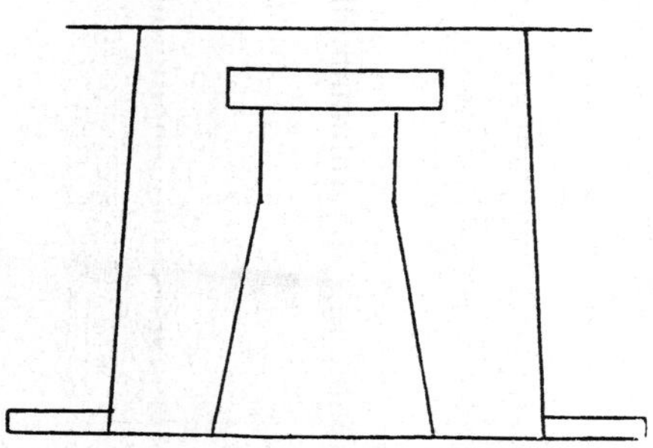

5.—SWEDISH, OR OSMUND, FURNACE.
("*Iron in Antiquity*," *Friend*.)

The great iron pillar of Delhi (the date of which is given by various authorities as B.C. 912 and A.D. 300) and the pillar of Dhar (A.D. 1304) are evidence of the high pitch to which the Hindus at an early period brought, and later maintained, the science and art of ironworking. It is extraordinary that while "rust doth corrupt" and has through many centuries slowly but surely corrupted most of the precious examples of the ironwork of antiquity, the Delhi column has been preserved intact. This has been said to be due to the grease from the naked bodies of natives who climb the pillar, or to the use of butter for anointing the pillar during ancient festivals ; but the favourable climatic conditions in India must also be taken into account.

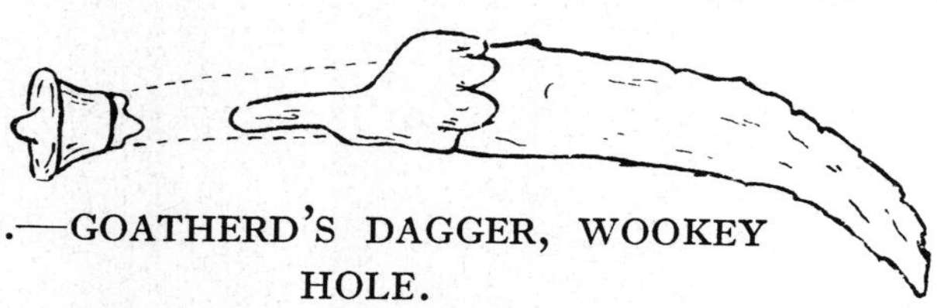

6.—GOATHERD'S DAGGER, WOOKEY HOLE.
("*Iron in Antiquity*," *Friend*.)

Modern science, however, has discovered that it is the sulphur content in iron which chiefly promotes rust, and that ancient charcoal iron, containing less sulphur than coke and coal iron, has always lasted proportionately longer. It is interesting to note, therefore, that, while the purest modern charcoal iron is 99.9 per cent. pure iron, the Delhi pillar is 99.72 per cent.

The early inhabitants of the Mesopotamian plain well knew the origin of their only source of iron, for their name for it means simply "heaven stone." This is an important fact, for it would seem to indicate that these people were late in discovering the properties of iron ore and the process of smelting, and that, in the opening stages of their civilisation, they drew their supplies entirely from meteoric iron.

Later in history we find that objects of iron of large size were buried in the tombs of the Sumerian nobility, together with pottery and other funerary furniture for the use of the departed spirit. The earliest important finds include a hammer, a spear and a saw from a tomb said to date from about 3000 B.C.

At the time when Nineveh was all-powerful the Assyrians were celebrated for their skill as ironworkers. The metal was used chiefly for defensive armour and door plates.

In contrast with Mesopotamia, we find that " heaven stone " was the later name for iron in Egypt, and the earliest finds are telluric, not meteoric.

Iron has been found in the Great Pyramid of Gizeh, and an almost contemporaneous find (significant only as evidence of the antiquity of ironworking) consisted of a large heap of iron rust from the early temple of Abydos.

It is now a definitely accepted fact that there was no sudden change or definite break in the continuity of Egyptian social development. There was no great catastrophe and no " Semitic Invasion." Recent discoveries form an unbroken chain of evidence. The earliest tombs contain flints and stone knives and implements, gradually improving in technique and as gradually displaced later on by copper, flint knives being retained only by the, as ever, conservative priesthood for symbolic and sacrificial purposes. The invention of bronze and then the discovery of iron can all be clearly traced from the discoveries recently made by Dr. Reisner.

It is now thought that the wall paintings in Egyptian tombs which represent bands of spearmen, some with spear-heads painted blue and others with weapons painted red, are intended to represent—the former the "shock troops," bearing iron-tipped arms, and the latter the " second line " troops armed with copper spear-heads.

The great Minoan civilisation was a bronze age culture, and iron was little known or used, for the opening of the iron age of the Cretan peoples was almost coincident with the decline of their civilisation.

The Greeks valued iron chiefly for its practical properties, particularly as a more efficient metal for tools. They did not develop, at first, the æsthetic possibilities of iron ; but in the remains at the Græco-Roman towns of Pompeii and Herculaneum can be seen wrought-iron window grilles and similar small examples of architectural ironwork.

7.—BRITISH CURRENCY BARS, FOUND WITH OTHERS AT HAM HILL, WINCHESTER, IN THE THAMES, AND AT OTHER PLACES. (*Victoria and Albert Museum.*)

The Romans also, like their forerunners, probably owing to their inability to master iron's tendency to rust, used it chiefly for tools and weapons, rather than in buildings. One of the most important finds dating from this period is the beak of a war vessel in the form of a ram, which was dredged up from the bed of the harbour at Genoa some years ago.

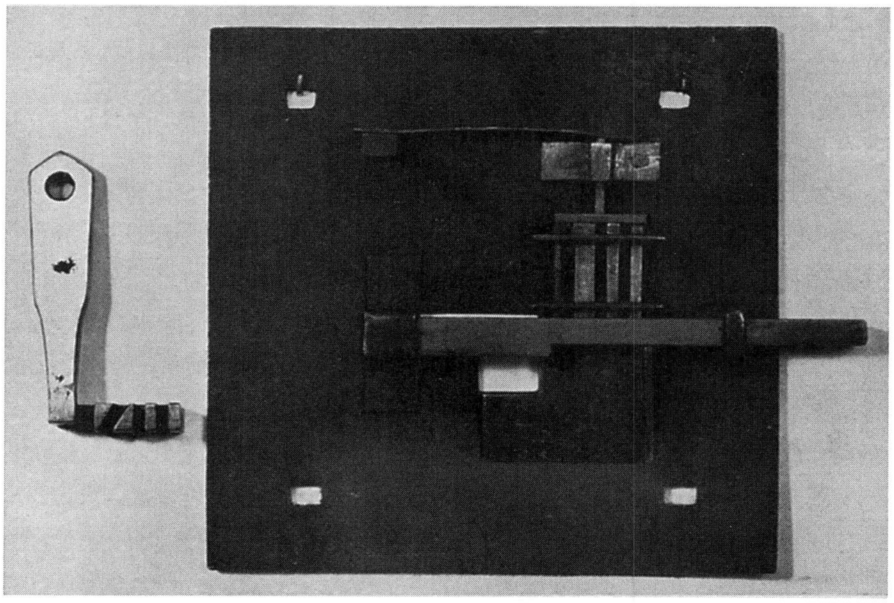

8.—MODEL OF A ROMAN LOCK AND KEY, SIMILAR TO ONE FOUND ON THE SAALBURG.
(*Victoria and Albert Museum.*)

From their histories we find that, at the time of Julius Cæsar, most of the semi-barbarous nations of Europe were acquainted with the working of iron and that their weapons showed evidence of extraordinary skill in the craft. Especially famous were the arms of the Spanish aborigines. In these histories we are also told that the art was well known in Britain, and Kipling, in his " Coming of the Steel " in *Rewards and Fairies*, gives a vivid picture of the way in which the use of iron may have spread in early times.

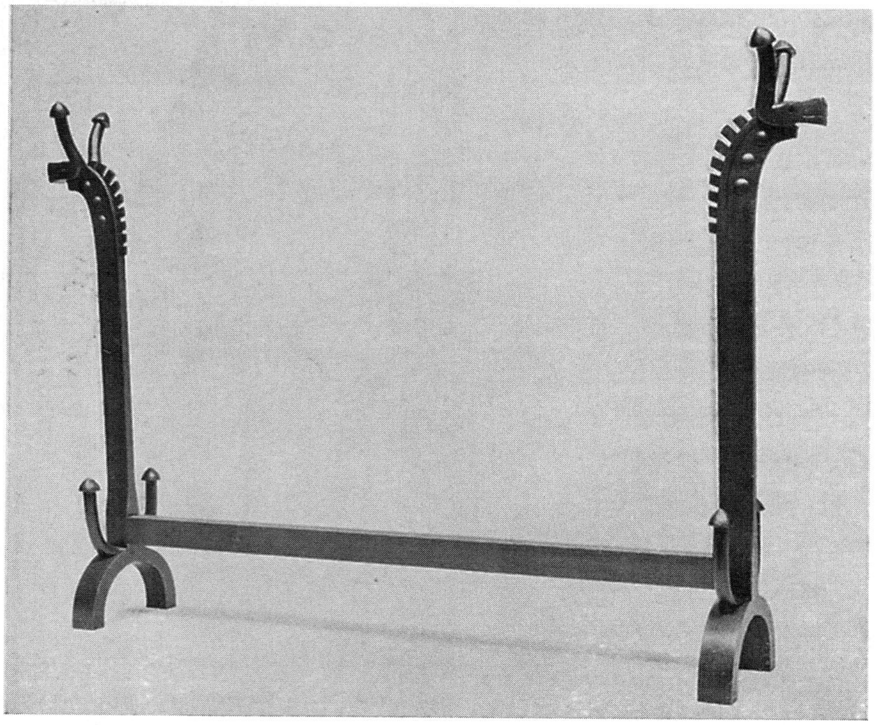

9.—ROMAN IRON FIRE-DOGS FOUND IN HERTFORDSHIRE.
(*British Museum.*)

Pre-Roman remains, consisting of iron rims for chariot wheels, sickles, keys, latch-lifters, saws, daggers, etc., have been found at Wookey Hole in Somerset, at Glastonbury and elsewhere. The early Britons used " currency bars " of iron before the introduction of coinage. These bars resembled short swords, and examples which have been discovered seem to show that the larger are simple multiples in weight of the smaller. Julius Cæsar saw and commented upon these bars.

It is only natural that most of the pre-Christian ironwork should either have been destroyed or have perished from oxidation, and that the few objects which remain to us should be largely eaten into and disfigured by rust. It must be remembered that all Europe became involved in the catastrophic conflagration in which Roman civilisation perished. We may, therefore, safely assume that, traditional forms being scanty, few iron objects produced before the fall of the Roman Empire had any appreciable influence on the design of similar objects produced after this date. Certainly the Romans influenced their subject races to a small extent; but Roman writers, in the main, agree that their European contemporaries, though "barbarians," generally equalled and often excelled their conquerors in the craft.

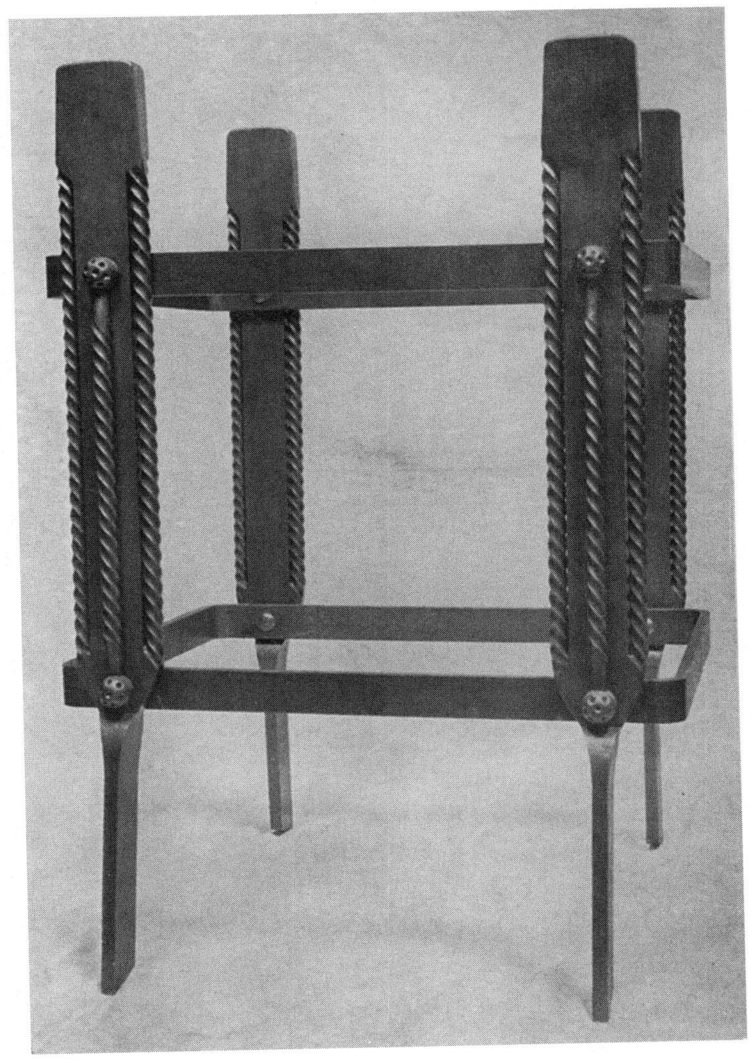

10.—ROMAN IRON FRAME (? ALTAR).
(British Museum.)

Being remote from the conflagration, the Goths became, unwittingly, the saviours of much of the Gallic and Roman tradition; though, in their hands, classic emblems were transformed into pagan devices, and gradually, in the course of centuries, grew almost unrecognisable.

In Britain, however, the arts languished, for the native tradition, fostered and moulded by the Romans, faded with their departure, and, though the Angles and Saxons in time settled in the lands they had conquered and introduced Scandinavian ideas and forms, they, strangely enough, did not develop the craft to any appreciable extent. On the other hand, they were soon strongly affected by Early Christian forms from Italy, which were brought over by St. Augustine and other missionaries. During the seventh century these influences were further complicated by the arrival of the Irish Christian missionaries with their Celtic traditions. The Irish and Roman priesthoods eventually joined forces, and their widely different art forms must have become fused with the existing style. This style was, therefore, being built up from very varied sources, most of which were coloured by Early Christian symbolism, for the Church at this time had already an international organisation.

The Danish Goths, however, provided the strongest impulse to the development of ironwork. In the ninth century these raiders began to settle on our coasts and intermarry with the

Anglo-Saxons. They are justly famed for their magnificent craftsmanship in metals, and a noteworthy feature of their work is the mingling of pagan with Christian symbolism.

Early English ironwork thus derived from two main sources: the Romano-British indigenous tradition and the importations from Scandinavia and Denmark. Illustrations of hinge-straps showing Danish influence appear in the Introduction, together with an account of the evolution of the hinge.

11.—BELLOWS DRIVEN BY WATER POWER, SIXTEENTH CENTURY. IN FOREGROUND SMALL WATER-HAMMER AND A MAN TEMPERING IN WATER.
(*From "Agricola."*)

We cannot do better than conclude with a quotation giving a very brief *résumé* of the history of ironwork in Britain from pre-Roman to mediæval times, which is interesting for the selection of points which the author stresses as important:

Iron has been worked in Britain from the earliest historical times, and flint implements have been found at Stainton-in-Furness and at Battle in Sussex in positions suggesting that ironworks may have existed in those places at the end of the Stone Age. Julius Cæsar relates that iron was produced along the coast of Britain, but only in small quantities, its rarity causing it to be considered as a precious metal, so that iron bars were current among the natives as money. The coming of the Romans soon changed this. They were not slow to see the value of the island's mineral wealth and to turn it to account. Ironworks sprang up all over the country: at Maresfield in Sussex they were apparently in full swing by the time of Vespasian (died A.D. 69), and in the neighbourhood of Battle fifty years later. Even more important were the workings in the West, on the banks of the Wye and in the Forest of Dean. Near Coleford have been found remains of Roman mines with shallow shafts and adits, while round Whitchurch, Goodrich, and Redbrook are enormous deposits of "cinders," or slag, dating from the same period. Ariconium, near Ross, was a city of smiths and forgemen; and Bath (Aquæ Sulis) is often said to have had a "collegium fabricensium," or gild of smiths, as one of its members, Julius Vitalis, armourer of the 20th Legion, dying after nine years' service, was given a public funeral here by a gild; but it seems more probable that the seat of the gild was at Chester, and that Julius had come to Bath for his health.

It is a most remarkable fact that although abundant circumstantial evidence of the Roman exploitation of British iron exists in the shape of coins and other relics found upon the site of the works, there is practically no trace of any such working during the Saxon period until shortly before the Conquest. The furnaces must have been still in blast when the Saxons landed; they were a warlike race, possessing a full appreciation of iron and something of the Scandinavian admiration for smithcraft, yet there is hardly a trace of their having worked iron in this country. Few, if any, objects definitely assignable to this period have been found upon the site of ironworks, and documentary evidence is almost non-existent. There is a charter of Oswy, King of Kent, given in 689, by which he grants to the Abbey of St. Peter of Canterbury land at Limings "in which there is known to be iron ore"; and there is the legend that about A.D. 700 Alcester, in Warwickshire, was the centre of busy ironworks, peopled with smiths, who, for their hardness of heart in refusing to listen to St. Egwin and endeavouring to drown his voice by beating on their anvils, were swallowed up by the earth; but the rest is silence, until we come to the time of Edward the Confessor. The Domesday Survey shows that in the time of the Confessor Gloucester rendered as part of its farm, 36 "dicres" of iron, probably in the form of horseshoes, and 100 rods suitable for making bolts for the king's ships, while from Pucklechurch in the same country came yearly 90 "blooms" of iron. The same Survey mentions that there were six smiths in Hereford, each of whom had yearly to make for the king 120 horseshoes; at Hessle, in the West

12.—OLD TYPE FURNACE, WITH FOOT-BLAST (ABOVE), AND BURCKHARD'S FURNACE, BLOWN BY WATER POWER (BELOW).

(*From original drawing in British Museum.*)

13.—EARLY WROUGHT IRON ON A WOODEN LECTERN.

Riding—one of the few Yorkshire manors which had increased in value between 1066 and 1086—it records six ironworkers, and it also refers to iron mines on the borders of Cheshire, in Sussex, and elsewhere.

During the twelfth century the industry appears to have expanded. In the North, at Egremont, we read of the grant of an iron mine to the monks of St. Bees, and at Denby a similar grant was made about 1180 by William Fitz-Osbert to the Cistercians of Byland, whose mining activities had already, ten years earlier, brought them into collision with their brethren of the neighbouring Abbey of Rievaulx. Still earlier, in 1161, Robert de Busli had given the monks of Kirkstead a site in Kimberworth for four forges—two for smelting and two for working iron—with the right to dig ore and to take dead wood for fuel. In the next generation

14.—DOOR AT STILLINGFLEET, SHOWING SCANDINAVIAN INFLUENCE.

15.—DOOR AT SKIPWITH, SHOWING SWASTIKA ORNAMENT.

they agreed to modify their rights, so that they would not dig in arable land unless it was lying fallow, they would fill up their trenches and would not cut down timber trees. In Derbyshire, towards the end of the century, Sir Walter de Abbetoft gave to the monks of Louth Park, wood at Birley in Brampton and two smithies, namely one bloomery and one forge, with the right to take beech and elm for fuel. But it was in the south-west that the greatest development took place. During the whole of this century the Forest of Dean was the centre of the iron industry, and played the part that Birmingham has played in more recent times. All through the reign of Henry II, the accounts of the sheriffs of Gloucester tell of a constant output of iron, both rough and manufactured, iron bars, nails, pickaxes, and hammers sent to Woodstock, Winchester, and Brill, where the king was carrying out extensive building operations, horseshoes supplied to the army, arrows and other warlike materials dispatched to France, spades, pickaxes, and other miners' tools provided for the Irish expedition of 1172, iron brought for the Crusade which Henry projected, but did not live to perform, and 50,000 horseshoes made for the actual Crusade of Richard I. Throughout the thirteenth century the Forest of Dean retained its practical monopoly of the English iron trade, so far at least as the southern counties were concerned, and during the whole of that time, members of the family of Malemort were employed at a forge near the castle of St. Briavels, turning out enormous stores of bolts for cross-bows and other war material. But a rival was now growing up in the Weald of Sussex and Kent. As early as 1254 the sheriff of Sussex had been called upon to provide 30,000 horseshoes and 60,000 nails, presumably of local manufacture, and in 1275 Master Henry of Lewes, who had been the king's chief smith for the past twenty years, purchased 406 iron rods (kiville) "in the Weald" for £16 17s. 11d., while a year or two later he obtained another 75 rods from the same source and paid £4 3s. 4d. "to a certain smith in the Weald for 100 iron rods."

The Wealden works had the advantage, a great advantage in the case of so heavy a material as iron, of nearness to London, and soon obtained a footing in the London markets with imported Spanish iron at the expense of

Gloucestershire, which at the beginning of the reign of Henry III had been sending its iron to Westminster and into Sussex. It must not be imagined that the northern counties were neglecting their mineral wealth all this time; they were, on the contrary, very active, and were exploiting their iron with vigour and success. On the lands of Peter de Brus in Cleveland in 1271 there were five small forges each valued at 10s., and two larger worth £4 each: these sums may not sound very imposing, but it must be borne in mind that the best land in that district was then worth only 1s. an acre. Twenty years later the forges belonging to Furness Abbey yielded a profit of £6 13s. 4d., as compared with a profit on flocks and herds of only £3 11s. 3d., and it is probable that the Abbey had at least forty forges then working on their lands. The great quantity of iron obtained at Furness also formed the most valuable part of the booty carried off by the Scots in their raid in 1316. But the large production of iron in the northern counties was absorbed by their own local requirements, and this was still more the case with the smaller quantities smelted in Northamptonshire and Rutland. Derbyshire must have been another important centre, for as early as 1257, four or five forges in the Belper ward of Duffield Frith were yielding about £10 each yearly, and, in 1314, two forges in Belper accounted for £63 6s. 8d. in thirty-four weeks, and there was a third, yielding nearly £7 10s. for only eleven weeks' work, but there is nothing to show that Derbyshire iron was ever sent south, and from the middle of the fourteenth century such English iron as was used in London was almost entirely drawn from the Weald.

In order to understand how Sussex and Kent, where no iron has been worked for the last hundred years, came to be the centres of a great iron industry in mediæval times, it must be borne in mind that charcoal was the only fuel used for iron working, until Dud Dudley discovered a method of using pit coal, about 1620, a date

16.—TWELFTH CENTURY DOOR AT STAPLEHURST.

17.—DOOR AT WORFIELD, SHOWING DUCKS AND EELS.

which may be considered to mark the end of the Mediæval period in iron mining.—(L. F. Salzman, M.A., F.S.A. *English Industries of the Middle Ages*, pages, 21–26.)

The convenience or necessity of dividing up the history of architecture chronologically or into styles and centuries inclines one to lose sight of the all-important transitional periods. The unwary are prone to regard the changes that occur as sudden inspirations of, possibly, one great designer, and forget the gradual building up of many years, with that final culmination in some great work which dramatically establishes a landmark in history to which all later designers gratefully look back.

It is, therefore, necessary to deal rather more fully than space in a historical note permits with the history of wrought ironwork in England from the tenth to the sixteenth centuries, before we approach the subject of the great output and rapid development in the work of the seventeenth and eighteenth centuries. The former period is dealt with in Chapters II and III.

CHAPTER II

INTRODUCTORY

WHILE there is evidence that the art of extracting and working iron in England was well established before the invasion of the Romans, the latter were the first to practise it largely, particularly in the Forest of Dean, Monmouthshire, and in the Weald of Sussex. Here, both in the time of the Romans and for many centuries after, charcoal from the surrounding woodlands supplied fuel for smelting the ores which the neighbourhood plentifully provided.

An account of the early process is given in the following quotation from Percy's well known work:

> From suitable ore, of which abundant and readily accessible supplies exist in various localities, nothing more easy can be conceived than the extraction of malleable iron—of all metallurgical processes it may be regarded as the most simple.
>
> Thus if a lump of red or brown hæmatite be heated for a few hours in a charcoal fire, well surrounded by, or embedded in, the fuel, it will be more or less completely reduced, so as to admit of being easily forged at a red heat into a bar of iron.—(*Metallurgy*, page 873.)

The method employed in the earliest times was the firing of a mound of ore and charcoal upon an open hearth; subsequently rude furnaces were introduced, with an artificial draught from bellows worked by manual labour. The heat produced by these furnaces was never great enough to reduce the iron to a liquid state, but merely to a lump of spongy consistency, from which the unburned ore and refuse were driven by means of hammering. The accompanying sketch section through a Catalan forge, taken from Dr. Percy's *Metallurgy*, shows the simplicity of the apparatus, and in writing of the Roman ironworks in Gloucestershire and Sussex he says:

> The metal was obtained direct from the ore in a malleable state with charcoal as fuel; and by a method no doubt closely resembling, if not identical with, the Catalan process.—(*Metallurgy*, page 876.)

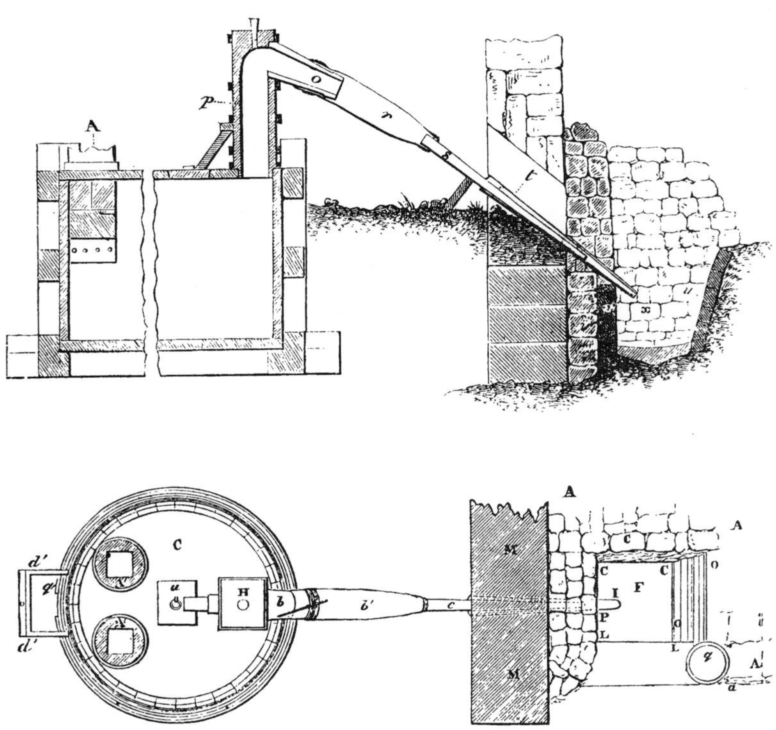

18.—PLAN AND SECTION OF A CATALAN FORGE.
("*Metallurgy*," *Percy*.)

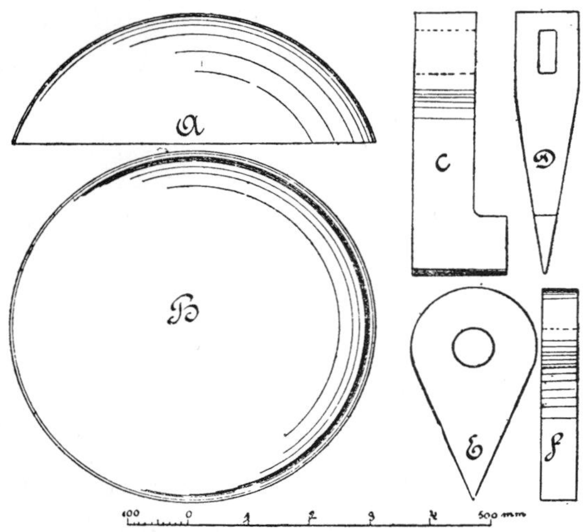

19.—"LOAF" TYPE OF BLOOM, WITH TOOLS USED IN DIVIDING.

A, *Elevation*; B, *plan*; C, D, *hammer*; E, F, *wedge*.

The lump of metal was re-heated and hammered under great hammers worked by a water-wheel fitted with buttons, which raised the hammers as they revolved and released them to fall again. This process was continued until the iron had become a solid rectangular mass called a bloom, in which state it was sold to the blacksmith.

> The term bloom . . . is clearly derived from the Saxon word *bloma*, which is defined by Bosworth as "metal, mass, lump." The ancient furnaces . . . were designated "*bloomeries*."—(Percy, *Metallurgy*, page 254.)

The subsequent labour entailed in forging these "blooms," until the smith had reduced them to bars and sheets ready for use, must have been enormous, but it was far from waste of labour. The nature of iron being fibrous, in order that it might be pliable under the hammer, it was necessary that these fibres should be interwoven in all directions to obtain perfect evenness of texture, and thus to ensure against the metal breaking or tearing when being moulded into shape. The conversion of the "blooms" met this requirement and at the same time contributed to its durability. To this durability must be added the natural durability of pure charcoal iron, compared with coke and coal iron with its high sulphur content. Charcoal iron does not readily rust, and, as can be seen on ancient decorative ironwork almost everywhere, it corrodes in a way that leaves a black coating of magnetic oxide which protects it indefinitely.

At the present day it is probably only in horseshoes that one finds wrought iron approaching the quality of that used prior to the fourteenth century, when the ironworks first began to supply iron to the smiths in rough bars more or less ready for use. Old horseshoes are invariably saved up and re-used, and the constant beating on the roads and subsequent re-forging together with the old nails, which are made from the toughest Swedish iron, eventually bring the iron up to the highest pitch of perfection.

Recently, in an interesting article on this subject, the statement was made that the Chinese, who are famous for the antiquity and excellence of their ironwork, now buy up old horseshoes from Great Britain for re-use in other forms in China.

Sir St. John Hope's history of Windsor Castle throws some light upon the subject of the weight and size of pieces or "blooms" of iron, which probably varied in different districts. One item, in an account for the Round Table during the reign of Edward III, reads as follows:

> for 27 pieces of iron bought for making and mending divers necessaries 6s 9d

—or 3d. apiece. An entry in an account dated January 1st, 1354–55, for 1,100lb. of iron for 66s., and, on March 12th of the same year, 1,003lb. of iron for 65s. 2½d., shows that the price of iron at that time was about ¾d. per pound. Thus, the weight of these particular pieces of iron must have averaged about 4lb.

Though there is one instance in the accounts of the purchase of 200 " esperducas " of iron, and two as merely " 200 of iron," in all other instances iron was bought by the pound weight until nearing the end of the fifteenth century, when we find an entry for " four *casks* of iron." From this it will be readily seen how laborious was the task of the smith in the preliminary stages of his work ; and one recognises the effect it had upon the general design of the day, for they rarely indulged in massive productions involving long, straight, heavy bars (save in windows) until the fifteenth century. Here, again, Sir St. John Hope's history of Windsor serves us well, for it gives us the price of the plain square window bars which filled every window of any importance. Items for " ironwork " to windows occur constantly ; among the first is one of interest of a purely homely character, dated August 11th, 1239, two months after the birth of Edward I, when a writ was issued " to cause the chamber of our son Edward to be wainscoated and iron bars to be made to each of the windows (*ibid.*, page 64)—probably the earliest recorded instance of the precautionary barring of a nursery window !

Smiths' wages in the middle of the fourteenth century ranged from 3½d. to 6d. a day, and a junior smith received 9d. a week—an entry occurs for the payment to John Smyth and his boy of 19s. 10d. for thirty-four days at 7d. for the two—and for " hinges etc to the door of the Canons' Chambers " he was only paid 4d. per day. In another account for a large quantity of heavy ironwork, which was probably for the portcullis and doors to a new gateway in course of erection in 1361, the price, including the iron, was 1¼d. per pound, or ½d. per pound for the labour.

At the same time several entries occur for " window iron " at a cost of 3d. per pound, or 2¼d. per pound after allowing for the iron. In 1355 John Smyth was paid 1d. per pound for eight bars of iron weighing 100lb., for the cloisters, "at task work," the King supplying the iron :

> And to John Smyth for making 8 bars of iron for the stone cloister, of the Kings iron weighing 100lbs

20.—HINGE BANDS AND STRAPWORK, FORMERLY ON THE SLYPE DOOR, SOUTH TRANSEPT, ST. ALBAN'S ABBEY. TWELFTH CENTURY. (*Victoria and Albert Museum.*)

taking per lb one penny at task work .. 8s. 4d
(*Ibid.*, page 156.)

21.—GRILLE FROM CHICHESTER CATHEDRAL. THIRTEENTH CENTURY.
(*Victoria and Albert Museum.*)

For the present purpose we may reasonably assume that these bars were $\frac{7}{8}$in. square, when they would weigh as near as possible $2\frac{1}{2}$lb. per foot. On this basis the total length of the bars must have been 40ft., or 5ft. each bar, and, taking the wages at 6d. per day, about 29ins. of $\frac{7}{8}$in. square bar represented a day's work! From this it will be seen that the labour entailed in the forging of bars was very heavy and, consequently, better paid than other ironwork, for in considering the wages paid per day one must remember that a day's work then meant anything up to about sixteen hours.

In 1394 it was enacted in London that, "by reason of the great nuisance, noise, and alarm experienced in divers ways by the neighbours," no smith should work henceforth "by night, but only from the beginning of daylight to nine of the clock at night throughout the whole of the year" (Ordinances of the Blacksmiths—articles dated eighteenth year, Richard II, A.D. 1394).

While from the foregoing we see that the price of straight bars was high, it was probably rather the excessive amount of labour than the cost which discouraged the use of it at that time. In describing the tomb of Queen Phillippa (*d.* 1369), the wife of Edward III, Mr. Francis Bond says:

> It is remarkable that instead of having new railings made to protect the tomb, the King bought the railings standing round the tomb of Michael, Bishop of London, outside the West Porch of St Pauls Cathedral.—These railings were merely plain straight bars, and the fact that Edward paid for them second-hand the great sum of £600 shews what a great achievement of craftsmanship it was considered to be to forge a straight and true bar.—(*Westminster Abbey*, page 232.)

The inference he draws is almost certainly wrong, and it is more probable that the enormous cost was due to other causes. The King may have been anxious to protect his wife's tomb immediately, and, possibly, "hush money" was demanded before the desecration of the bishop's tomb could be conveniently accomplished.

It is curious that, while the illuminated manuscripts of the tenth and eleventh centuries show hinges and other ironwork of the light and ornamental character which we find only in actual pieces that we know to be of the thirteenth and fourteenth centuries, the only work of

22.—AUMBRY DOORS, CHESTER CATHEDRAL.

the earlier periods which remains with us is of a much cruder type, in which naturalistic forms and foliage were rarely introduced. In *Domestic Architecture in England*, from which the accompanying illustrations have been taken, this point is referred to as follows :

> If we are to rely upon the authority of these ancient drawings, the ironwork on the hall-doors was as florid and luxuriant in design as such work undoubtedly was in the thirteenth and fourteenth centuries ; . . . . . Unfortunately the drawings in Saxon manuscripts cannot be entirely depended on as accurate delineations of contemporary architecture, ecclesiastical or domestic. Notwithstanding the great difference in style perceptible among them, it is obvious that the artists generally worked after certain admitted standards of design, which seem to have been furnished originally by the Greek school, to which later additions were made from time to time. This conventional style of drawing lasted till the twelfth century ; and there is little difference between architectural details in works of that age and those that occur in writings two centuries older. . . . Still although too much credit must not be given to early illuminations they frequently present minor details from objects which surrounded them.—(Vol. I, page xv.)

And again :

> From an early period, in fact from the 10th century, it may be remarked that in all drawings and paintings in manuscripts ironwork on doors presents an ornamental character : the bars of the hinges project almost entirely across the panel and are more or less floriated. The scutcheons of the locks are frequently ornamental. . . .(*Ibid.*, Chapter I, page 10.)

It is probable that much of the earlier ironwork was taken from its original doors, etc., and re-forged into fresh shapes ; but, upon the whole, it would appear likely that these drawings display the conventional method of representing ironwork rather than illustrations of the actual work of the period.

Decorative ironwork anterior to the thirteenth century was used chiefly in conjunction with wood, in the form of hinges or elaborate coverings to doors, chests, etc., to strengthen and render them defensive. The designs were almost invariably geometrical and purely conventional in character, representing curious nuptic signs, dragons, swastikas, birds, beasts and ships. The most characteristic form of early hinge was that of the crescent bisected by a bar extending beyond the horns of the crescent. The spaces between the hinges were frequently covered with separate pieces of ornamental ironwork and bars with branching scrolls. In some instances there does not appear to have been much consideration given to the effect produced upon the door as a whole, the different pieces having, apparently, little or no relation one to the other (as at Stillingfleet Church in Yorkshire), whereas in other cases the entire door was covered with one complete and elaborate geometrical figure.

Mr. ffoulkes, in his recent work on *Decorative Ironwork*, has devoted a section to hinges, in which he traces most clearly the development from the earliest type to the profusely decorated work of the later periods (*Decorative Ironwork from the XI to the XVIII Century*).

23.—WEST DOOR, HENRY III CHAPEL, WINDSOR.

24.—CHAPTER HOUSE DOOR, YORK MINSTER.

There is an exceedingly interesting door to the vestry at Tewkesbury Abbey, completely covered on the inside with roughly beaten-out iron plates about one-sixteenth of an inch thick, and averaging 20ins. long and $4\frac{1}{2}$ins. wide, nailed to the oak door, which is further strengthened, and the plates more firmly kept in place, by a flat iron frame 2ins. wide by $\frac{1}{4}$in. thick. This frame runs right round the outer edge of the door, and connected with it are vertical, horizontal and diagonal bands of the same width and thickness ; the whole are laid over the iron plating and bolted right through the door. The plates, which are of irregular shapes, are laid slightly overlapping and with no attempt at a pattern. The ring handle on the outside is of later date than the door, and will be referred to again. The door would appear to be of the thirteenth century.

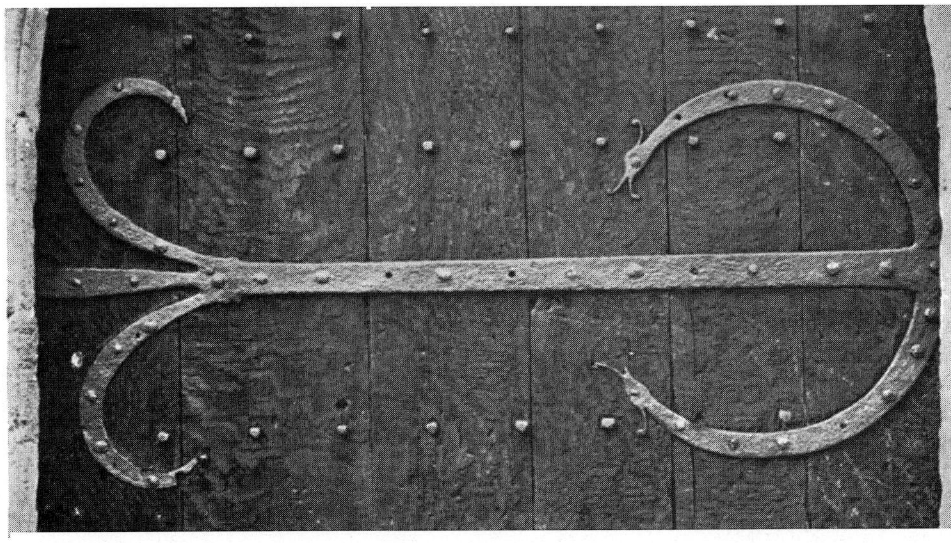

25.—AN EARLY FORM OF HINGE-STRAP AT STOKE ORCHARD.

Mr. Starkie Gardner, in *English Ironwork*, mentions a similar door in the crypt under the Chapter House at Wells, which he describes as—

> a most interesting thirteenth century door completely sheathed externally with iron, reinforced with decorative straps intersecting at various angles. Evelyn, visiting Bury St. Edmunds in 1672, observed " the gates are wood but quite plated over with iron," yet examples of this are so rare that it could at no period have been a general practice with us.—(*English Ironwork of the XVII and XVIII Centuries*, page 3.)

The Rev. E. F. Smith, the Vicar of Tewkesbury, has kindly furnished a local tradition regarding this door, which is that the iron plates covering it are composed of armour and swords used in the Battle of Tewkesbury, May 4th, 1471. They are supposed to have been beaten out by the monks and used in this way as a memorial to the fighting which took place on that occasion in the nave of the abbey church, the five western bays of which were at that time used as the parish church. This should probably be regarded in the light of a legend rather than a fact. One can certainly observe no indication from the shapes of the plates that they had been formed from pieces of armour.

The earliest open screen or grille remaining in England is that which formerly enclosed the shrine of St. Swithin in Winchester Cathedral, portions of which are now placed on the inner side of the north-west door. Mr. Starkie Gardner gives the date of this screen as 1093 (*Ironwork from the Earliest Times to the end of the Mediæval Period*, Part I, page 64). It may, however, be a little later—the reproduction

26.—TWELFTH CENTURY DOOR HINGE AT EARLS CROOME.

of a portion of it in the Victoria and Albert Museum is, indeed, labelled twelfth century. Like all the open ironwork at that time and up to the end of the thirteenth century, the screen consists merely of a flat iron frame filled in with light scrollwork of little or no constructional value. The method of connecting the scrolls to each other and to the frame was not by forging the scrolls themselves, but by binding or tying them together by means of light iron bands or collars forged and welded. Unfortunately, while there must at one time have been many screens of this type protecting the tombs and shrines in the churches and cathedrals all over the country, only those mentioned remain.

Both in the screen at Winchester and at Lincoln, and again in the thirteenth century grille from Chichester Cathedral (now in the Victoria and Albert Museum), there is the same feeling of frailness and lack of that rigidity which is essential to the proper use of wrought iron. Diaper patterns such as these remind one forcibly of painted mural decoration and, as gates and screens, fail to satisfy the eye. It would appear that the smith was troubled by the loss of the stiff oak backing upon which he had for so long been accustomed to rely, and had not as yet worked out for himself a fresh mode of design and construction to meet the new conditions. We shall see how this demand for open gates rather than for armoured doors was met, and how consequent developments affected every branch of the smiths' work. Before dealing with this, however, we have before us a school of smith work which culminated with the close of the thirteenth century. Standing out above all other schools of pure smithing, this period saw a pitch of excellence attained which remained supreme and unrivalled.

27.—HINGE-STRAP FROM MAXSTOKE PRIORY.

The development of Gothic architecture during the thirteenth century, resulting from the decreasing necessity for defensive design, had a naturally refining influence upon all trades, and in none more noticeably than the smiths. The introducing of more or less naturalistic forms of foliage—which, by their trailing lines and graceful curves, lent themselves readily to the imaginative faculties of the designers—produced eventually a beautiful type of ironwork. The examples still remaining closely resemble one another—so closely, indeed, that it has been suggested by many writers that several of those illustrated here must have been by the same hand. One remarkable example is the west door of Henry III's Chapel at Windsor (Fig. 23). In describing the west wall Sir St. John Hope said :

> But the innermost order of the middle arch is that of a doorway 5ft. 5½ inches wide and still retaining a pair of old doors covered with magnificent contemporary ironwork, disposed in scrolls all over the surface. In several places among this is a pointed oval with the name GILEBERTVS, of the smith who wrought the work.—(*Windsor Castle*, Vol. II, page 409.)

There have been various opinions expressed as to the meaning of this stamped name. Mr. ffoulkes writes :

> This stamp is also found on some crampons which are the sole remaining portions of the grille around the tomb of Henry III at Westminster Abbey,

and suggests that the stamp may possibly refer to Gilbert de Tile, who was " bailiff of Windsor at the end of the 13th century."

28.—DECORATIVE WORK AT UFFINGTON, BERKS.

29.—THIRTEENTH CENTURY DOOR AT FARINGDON, BERKS.

Search has not revealed these crampons with the stamp at Westminster ; but in the wardrobe book of Edward I there is a record of a payment in 1290 to Master Henry of Lewes for the ironwork of " the tomb of King Henry " (*Manners and Household Expenses, 13th and 15th Century*, Roxburghe Club, No. 57).

Mr. Lethaby also suggests that Henry of Lewes carried out both pieces of work, but he does not mention the presence of the " Gilebertvs " stamp on the fragments of the ironwork remaining on Henry III's tomb in Westminster (*Westminster Abbey and Craftsmen*, page 305).

It is most exasperating that the ancient accounts of Windsor Castle, which are so complete in other respects, omit in every instance to give definite information as to the smiths who made the various unique pieces of work still remaining there, and which will be referred to later.

It will be noticed that this ironwork has no connection with the hinges of the door; its sole duty is to bind together and stiffen the door. As a piece of design it undoubtedly holds the first place among the examples of this period. The spaces both within and between the three lozenges forming the main lines of the design are beautifully filled, and the graceful sweep of the

30.—DOOR AT MORVILLE, SHROPSHIRE.

31.—DOOR AT WELLS CATHEDRAL.

curves is maintained in this piece of work to a remarkable degree. In other examples it will be seen that the curves of the scrolls where they leave the main stem, and again in the subsidiary scrolls, tendrils and leaves, the flow of the line is frequently broken and interrupted, usually due to bad workmanship rather than to a fault in the design. This door, however, is almost entirely free from this: the main scroll corresponding to the one which encloses the handle plate has two unpleasant little sprigs striking out unnaturally at right angles to the main scroll, but this is the only unworthy note in the whole.

The point of greatest importance to be noticed in this and other examples illustrated here is the method employed by the smith in forming the leaves, flowers, bunches of grapes, etc. A close examination discloses that these were not modelled by blows from the hammer, but were produced from swages or dies cut out of tempered iron, into which the iron was hammered while hot —practically the same process as that of taking an impression from a seal. This and the beautifully modelled stems of the whorls and branches, for which moulding irons of different sections were used, are the chief characteristic features of ironwork of the end of the thirteenth century.

32.—THIRTEENTH CENTURY HINGE AT WHEATENHURST.

In a schedule and valuation of the stock of an ironmonger's shop, dated 1358, there is an item of " 33 pairs of okees, 6s." (*Appraisement of the goods and chattels of Stephen le Northerne* 30 Edward III, A.D. 1356, Letter Book G, folio xiv, Latin), which, as Mr. H. T. Riley suggests (*Memorials of London and London Life in the 13th, 14th & 15th Centuries*, page 282), may have meant *ogees*, the technical term for an S-shaped moulding. It will also be noticed that the leaves and flowers spring invariably from the outer side of the scrolls, another feature common to nearly all designs of this time.

In the covering to the aumbry doors in the Canons' Vestry in Chester Cathedral is another example, chiefly remarkable, perhaps, for its extreme lightness and delicacy. The total width of the three doors is 5ft. 7ins., and they are 4ft. 10½ins. in height. The scrolls and centre stem of the middle door are triangular in section, and in no part do they exceed half an inch in width, while they diminish in places to a bare eighth of an inch, gradually losing their angular section and becoming more rounded as they become smaller. The vertical detached ribs running up the sides of the left-hand door and the frame of the centre door are of half-round section. The door on the right is divided into two, the ironwork covering the upper half being the more carefully finished portion of the whole work. A very unusual feature is that the ends of the whorls or scrolls divide and curl right and left, with a centre leaf completing the scroll at a tangent to the natural sweep. The three lower pairs of scrolls to the centre panel are greatly disfigured by the addition of a leaf or tendril deliberately forged on in the opposite direction to the growth of the vine. The flower-like ends bisecting the main

33.—HINGE-WORK AT ABBEY DORE.

scrolls on the left-hand door and upon the two on the right are particularly beautiful, and recall to one's mind the grace and delicacy of the Grecian honeysuckle. The faulty broken curves, absent in the door to Henry III's chapel, are here very marked, both in the drooping tendril from the uppermost scroll, which runs down the hinge side of the left door, and again on the centre door, at the intersection of the two top scrolls before they commence to curl. It will be noticed in several places, particularly at the junctions of the scrolls with the main vertical stem in the centre door, that there is a leaf superimposed, and a second leaf curls back and hangs down towards one. This is not found in the Windsor door, and is a refinement

34.—QUEEN ELEANOR'S GRILLE, WESTMINSTER ABBEY.

of smithing which, while being ornamental, has also a definite object. An examination of the illustration will show that at each point where a scroll or leaf stalk springs from the main stem there is a swelling and flattening of the iron. This is due to the process of welding one piece to the other, which, without distorting the section of the iron at the welding point, is a difficult feat to accomplish. These covering leaves, then, were added to conceal this joint and so maintain the easy flow of the design without interruption.

The inner sides of the doors to the Chapter House, York Minster, present another interesting example, though poor in design compared with the two already described. The complete vine plant is represented, including the root, and finishing with a flower, on each side of which are curious winged dragons. Here, again, the scrolls end in a flower and two leaves and, as at Windsor, the first whorl of one scroll encircles the handle plate, which, in this instance, is cruciform and very large, with an open basket in bold relief to take the drop handle, now missing. The section of the main stems is, in this case, that of two rounded beads. The welding points at the junction of the main scrolls and where the first scrolls leave the main stem are treated quite conventionally with a moulded cross-piece or base. Only at the junction of the third pair of scrolls with the main stem, and again where the stem ends in the topmost flower and tendrils, do covering leaves occur.

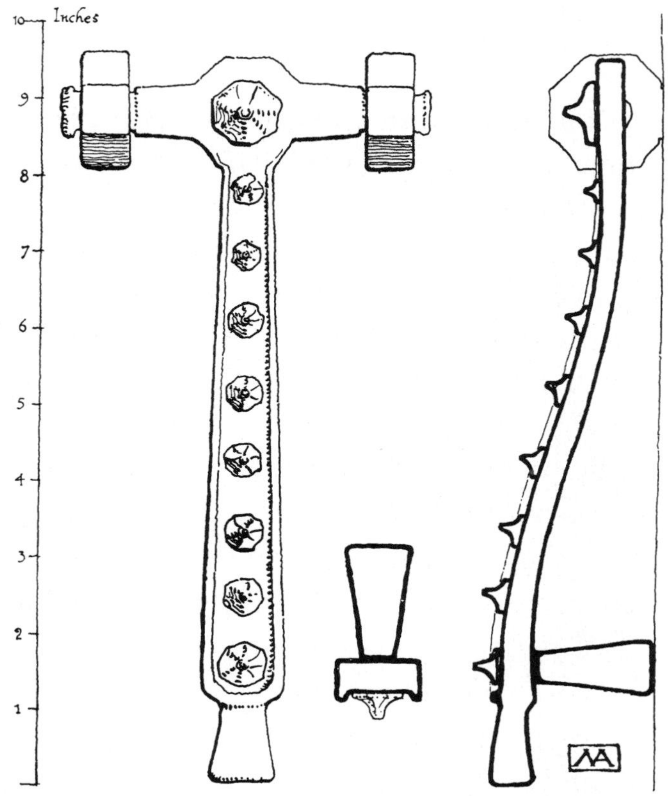

35.—KNOCKER, WEST GATE, CANTERBURY CATHEDRAL.

However, by far the most magnificent piece of work of this period still left to us is the grille or grate in Westminster Abbey to the tomb of Eleanor of Castile, wife of Edward I. In it we find every detail characteristic of this manner represented in such perfection as to render the whole grille unique and unrivalled in Europe. There is no other instance of open ironwork of this type, all other remaining examples being coverings to doors, chests, etc., similar to those already described. To add to its interest, the records concerning its manufacture and the name of the actual smith are preserved in the accounts of the executors of Queen Eleanor. These are in Latin, and are of such great interest as to justify their being given in full. They read as follows :

Payments made from the monies of the Lady Eleanor Queen Consort by J. Bacun and R. Myddleton from the term of St. Michael at the end of the 21st year of King Edward (1294)

Tomb. Item to Master Thomas de Leghtone, smith, in part payment 12 li for making the ironwork round the tomb of the Queen at Westminster .. .. lx.s

Tomb. Item to Master Thomas de Leghtone, smith, for making the ironwork round the tomb of the Queen, in part payment xij marks .. .. lx.s

Payments. for the Queen Consort from the term of St. Hilary in the 22nd year of King Edward.

Tomb. Item on the following Sunday to Master Thomas de Leghtone in part payment of xij li for the making of the ironwork round the Queen's Tomb .. .. xx.s

Item on the following Wednesday to the same Thomas de Leghtone in final settlement of xlj. li for the making of the aforesaid ironwork and for the carriage of the same from Leghtone as far as London and the expenses of the aforesaid Thomas and his men while they stayed in London for placing and setting the same ironwork by the Tomb .. .. vl. li

It has been suggested by Sir Matthew Wyatt, in his book, *Metalwork*, that Thomas de Leghtone was Thomas of Leighton Buzzard, his ground for this being the similarity of the workmanship to that of the fine hinges on the door of the parish church at Leighton Buzzard. As Mr. Burgess points out, the grille does not appear to have been designed so much for the protection of the tomb—

> as to prevent ill-disposed persons from getting into the Confessors Chapel by climbing over the effigy ;

and he goes on to say that the security of the chapel—

> was doubtless effected in the first instance by high and close grilles, which went all round between the pillars of the Chapel. . . . Now when Henry III and Queen Eleanor's tombs were erected, these high grilles were necessarily removed, and the tombs being very lofty, at least on the ambulatory side, the only precaution necessary was to devise some means of preventing the evilly disposed from climbing over.—(*Westminster Abbey*, by G. G. Scott and others.)

The main frame consists of two plain flat horizontal bars, the lower one and the upper one, connected together at regular intervals by curved upright bars which divide the grille into eleven panels, again subdivided by central bars of lighter section. Each of these bars is beautifully moulded. They are turned over, riveted and welded at each end to the main horizontal bars, the welded joint being, in each case, concealed behind a rose or leaf, and in five cases by well modelled wolves' heads. The uprights are carried on above the top bar and terminate in tridents, in four of which the centre prong is forked, and in one the side prongs also. It is probable that these tridents did duty as pricket candlesticks at times of special festivals. In the Windsor Castle accounts relating to the chapel during the last years of the thirteenth century there is an item of 12d. paid to the smith—

> for 26 prickets of iron made for putting candles on in the Chapel of the Castle, by the King's order.

Altogether, from a practical point of view, it is excellently constructed, and forms a most efficient guard against intrusion into the chapel.

The unevenness and variation resulting from stamped or punched ornament renders the repetition of the use of few dies hardly discernible. On examining the grille very closely, one can find only two varieties of roses and different leaves. The upright bars behind the floral scrolls are beautifully moulded with moulding irons, and, in addition, are all enriched to a degree that is astonishing by stamping and chisel marks. In the larger bars Mr. Burgess draws attention to a curious form of ornament in the shape of—

> little studs or nails inserted at regular intervals and rivetted on the back.

One can find the same ornament on the knocker to a door in the West Gate, Canterbury Cathedral, and it is, so far as we are aware, an uncommon form of decoration.

We have already explained, in describing the ironwork at Chester Cathedral, the reason for the covering leaves at the junction between one piece of iron and another : there, it will be remembered, these occurred in a few instances only. In the Eleanor grille every welding point throughout is concealed in this manner ; yet, so beautifully has the design been worked out that the smith has successfully concealed his own cleverness ; and in no instance is there any apparent effort in the arrangement of the foliage. The arrangement of the eleven panels which make up the grille is curious. Each panel varies in some slight degree ; two only are distinctly different, but are exactly similar each to the other. They are the fifth and eighth, reading from left to right, and they carry tridents very much smaller than those to the other panels. These two were probably put in later to replace tridents broken by robbers attempting to rifle the tomb. To the modern mind such an arrangement is inconceivable, for one would naturally place these two panels equidistant from the centre, say fifth and seventh or fourth and eighth, and to do otherwise would be rightly condemned as affectation. On the other hand, it is this childlike disregard for symmetry and order which lends much charm to the early work. Such lapses become more and more rare as time advances, and the education which minimised them was too often accompanied by loss of individuality and life.

There is a fine chest at Westminster, noted by Mr. Burgess, whose illustrations are reproduced here, which, he states, comes from the Chapel of the Pyx. It is of fine workmanship, and may well have been made by Thomas de Leghtone or Henry of Lewes. In the parish church in the

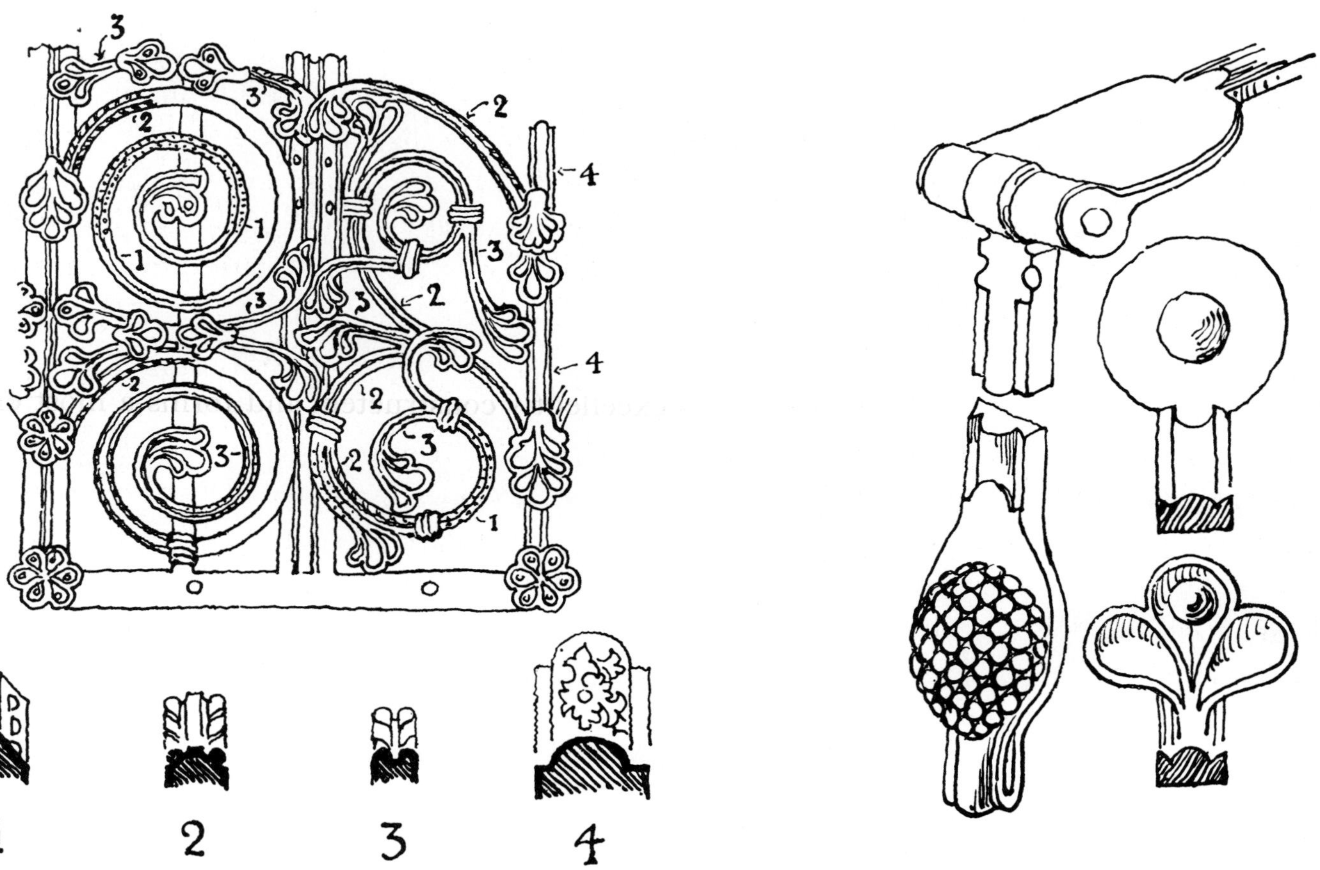

36.—DETAILS OF WROUGHT IRONWORK ON CHEST, WESTMINSTER ABBEY.

village of Malpas, Cheshire, about fifteen miles from Chester, there is another magnificent chest profusely covered with ironwork. Its special interest lies in its undoubted inspiration by the aumbry doors at Chester Cathedral. Here we have an effort on the part of the smith to reproduce the effect of stamped ornament without the aid of dies or punches. The whole of this work is the result of the hammer only. It will be seen that many of the junctions between stalks and stems have the covering leaf, and, while there is great charm in the complete work, the smithing and design, if it can be designated as such, is of the clumsiest description when compared with that which it aspired to emulate.

And thus the thirteenth century drew to a brilliant close, and with it one of the most glorious periods in the history of architecture, for the smiths, in their great effort, were only keeping in line with other trades in one inspired movement forward, which culminated, in their case, with the work of Thomas de Leghtone and others like him.

It is not possible to say how far this early work was designed prior to its entering upon the actual course of construction, probably only in a very general way, to be elaborated and altered by the smith during the progress of execution. It certainly bears all the signs of this being the case, for sudden changes of pattern to meet unforeseen difficulties, tightening

37.—OAK CHEST, MALPAS CHURCH, CHESHIRE.

up or widening out curves and scrolls, and so on, all go to show that the smith worked with great freedom once the main lines, for which he may or may not have been directly responsible, were settled.

The very generally accepted theory that each workman designed and carried out his own particular work on a building, untrammelled by the instructions of a leading mind, is open to serious doubt. Orders for work—be it stone, woodwork, iron or what you will—had to be given by some one person in charge of the building as a whole, and it is unlikely that, in giving such orders, instructions as to the general lines to be adopted should not have been given also.

There are other examples of thirteenth century ironwork in the country—Mr. Starkie Gardner mentions fourteen as the total number—but those illustrated here are sufficient to give the reader a clear idea of the characteristics common to all. It is impossible wholly to agree with Mr. Starkie Gardner's summing up of these. He writes :

> All the work has certain characteristics in common ; thus it is all are formed of easy scrolls, flowing one from the other *and which rarely complete a second whorl.*—(*Ironwork*, pages 76–77.)

Nevertheless, the examples at Chester, Windsor, Westminster and York all have scrolls formed of two, two and a half and three whorls. Nor, again, are " dragons heads introduced in all " (*ibid.*). The main features are, however, so marked as to render it unnecessary to describe the details, which, in each example, vary in some degree. Before proceeding to the work which developed during the fourteenth century, it is essential to realise that, up to the end of the thirteenth century, the entire manipulation of the iron was carried out while at welding heat—that is, red hot ! It will be clear that this was so by the forms adopted, which are all of a flowing character most easily wrought in a material pliant with heat. There is no doubt that this is the most natural and reasonable method for the production of decorative ironwork. Calling, as it does, for great quickness of eye and dexterity of hand, it of necessity brings out to the full the individuality of the worker, and the fact that, during the actual progress of the modelling and working, the iron is red hot renders dead accuracy in repetition practically impossible. There is, therefore, invariably a freedom and directness which, in combination with simplicity and breadth of form, gives a greater charm and interest to wrought iron than to almost any other art of that period, for in no other does one find vigour and daintiness allied to the same extent.

CHAPTER III

FOURTEENTH TO SEVENTEENTH CENTURIES

WITH the fourteenth century came a practical cessation of all decorative ironwork, and not until the beginning of the fifteenth century did it again begin to reappear. Architecture, in the meantime, had developed along lines which demanded changes in the methods of workmanship, since the gradually increasing fondness for regularity, repetition and symmetry in design could not be coped with by the methods hitherto employed. After this long interval of inactivity we find work growing up of so entirely different a character as to render a comparison of the merits of one with the other impossible.

It has already been pointed out that the design of wrought ironwork necessarily advanced with that of all the allied arts, and it is a matter for congratulation that the smiths adapted themselves to the prevailing fashion. To have attempted to carry out the work required of them by the means used by Thomas de Leghtone would have spelled failure, and the consequent disuse of their services in decorative work. We find, therefore, an ever increasing adoption of the constructional methods employed in woodwork : iron lending itself as readily to these as to the forge and anvil. It may be sawn, cut, and framed together when cold exactly as though it were a hard wood, and, being free from grain, knots and the natural defects to which timber is subject, it is admirably adapted for such treatment, while, at the same time, it retains this advantage over wood, that it may be forged at any point desired.

Plate iron was used, largely pierced into open tracery patterns, one sheet placed over another to obtain different planes, or cut and forged into endless varieties of thin mouldings to be riveted to the face of plain bars. Solid iron was cut into the most delicate architectural forms with an accuracy and command unsurpassed in any other material ; indeed, we find even the complete human figure essayed and accomplished. It is impossible, therefore, to agree with Mr. Charles ffoulkes' implied condemnation of the smiths in altering their methods to meet new demands, when he writes :

> The halving and mortising of iron bars can hardly be regarded as smiths work, for it belongs rather to the domain of the carpenter and is seldom found in work that is representative of the smith at his best.—(*Decorative Ironwork*, page xxv.)

It is the part of every good workman to produce what is required of him in the best possible manner —to do otherwise is merely to stultify himself and eventually to lose his place among the craftsmen of other trades. It will be agreed that the finest examples of the thirteenth century and those of fifteenth century " benchwork " (the technical term for iron worked upon when cold) both attained perfection in their respective methods of workmanship, and this is the only fair way in which they can be subjected to comparison.

Of the fourteenth century we have practically no authentic examples. There is a charming pair of gates now in the Victoria and Albert Museum which were originally in Chichester Cathedral, but, though the exact date of these is unknown, they are, evidently, late fourteenth century or early fifteenth century work. Here we find the bars are all "halved" where they intersect—that is, half the substance of each bar is cut away to receive the half of the other, These bars form small square panels, each of which contains a simple quatrefoil. The whole is paired and riveted together without the aid of welding at any point.

The earliest screen of this period showing the fuller development of the new methods of construction is that which encloses the Chantry of Henry V in Westminster Abbey. This was made, as stated by Mr. Lethaby, by Roger Johnson of London—

> who in 1431 was ordered to arrest (press) smiths to complete the ironwork of the tomb of the late King.—(*Westminster Abbey and Craftsmen.*)

It is an excellent example of early iron tracery work, and an examination of the detail drawing in Fig. 38 will show how far removed it is from the ironwork previously discussed. The detail is by the late Mr. Burgess, who was probably able to determine the actual construction during some repair of the screen. By it one is able to see how carefully the whole is fitted and framed together, and that, beyond the preliminary forging of the bars and plates to the sizes and shapes required, there was little further work done at welding heat. The main uprights A are slightly rebated or sunk to receive B, the second member of the main mullions and semicircular heads, to the face of which is riveted a circular bar D. The horizontal and diagonal members B are halved and tenoned together, and in the centre are pierced and beaten out to form the main fillet of the trefoils which fill the design; C is the thin plate iron riveted to the back of the frame, also pierced to give the second or inner fillet of the trefoils. The construction, in fact, resembles very closely that of a good piece of *modern* wood trellis—the word "modern" is used advisedly, for at that time such woodwork was invariably cut out of the solid, the elaborate building up of joinery to overcome shrinkage and twisting being a comparatively modern achievement.

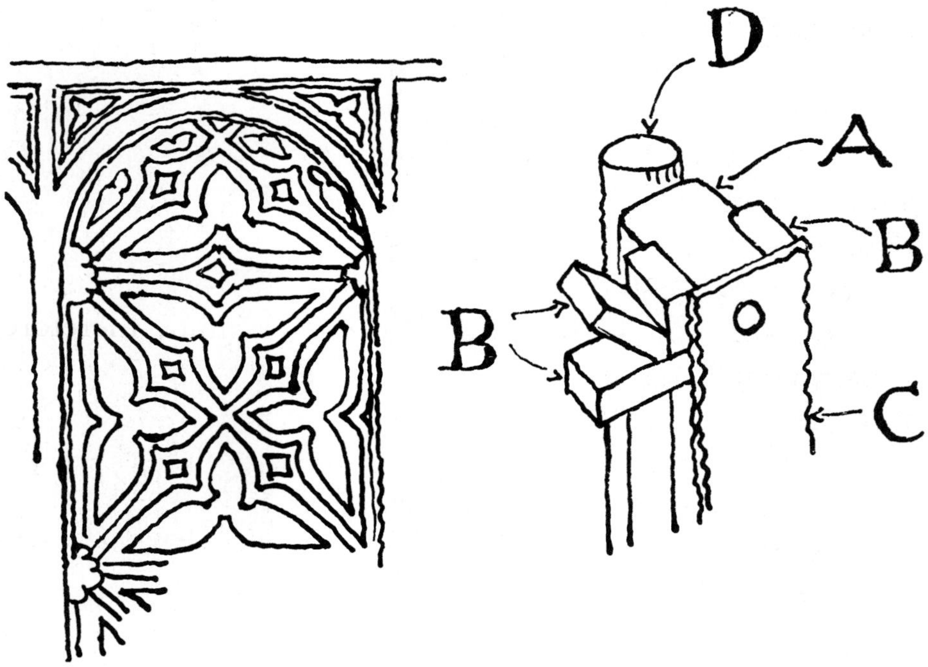

38.—DETAIL OF SCREEN, CHANTRY OF HENRY V CHAPEL, WESTMINSTER ABBEY.

A distinct branch of ironwork developed during the fourteenth century, in the form of protective railings to tombs and chantries, quite unlike the delicate screens and grilles of the preceding period, their general characteristic being strength and utility, to which decorative invention was subservient. It may be presumed that every tomb and effigy of any importance was at this time guarded by railings, the large majority of which were removed as the necessity for them passed away. With variations in details, these railings resemble one another closely. Composed of a series of stout vertical bars which are let in or tenoned at the bottom to a wide,

39.—DETAIL OF IRON RAILING TO TOMB OF THE SEVENTH EARL, FITZALAN CHAPEL, ARUNDEL CASTLE.

40.—SCREEN TO THE URSWICK CHANTRY, ST. GEORGE'S CHAPEL, WINDSOR.

flat bar resting on the paving or, in some instances, let into the paving itself, they run at the top through another bar, above which they finish as spikes. For decoration the smiths relied chiefly upon the treatment of this top bar, the main standards and the spikes or finishing of the ordinary bars. The top bar usually takes the form of a cresting, with more or less elaborately moulded side pieces riveted on and frequently battlemented and enriched by inscriptions or the application of pateræ, crests and rosettes. The main angle standards, emphasising the corners and dividing up long lengths of rail into bays, were stiffened by tall, elegant buttresses with weatherings and bases, following in detail the stonework of the period. On plan the vertical bars were frequently set diagonally and, above the horizontal top bar, either tapered away in long plain spikes or beaten out to flat spear-heads of various shapes. Though we may presume that guard rails were

42.—FARLEIGH HUNGERFORD CASTLE, TOMBS OF THE HUNGERFORDS IN THE CHAPEL.

41.—PORTION OF SCREEN, ST. GEORGE'S CHAPEL, WINDSOR.

in use from the beginning of the century, the earliest, probably, remaining in England are those which surround the tomb of Archbishop Langton, who was buried in Westminster Abbey in 1379. They are of a very simple type, and so is the cresting, which is formed of moulded plates inside and out, 3½ins. deep. The vertical bars are square and continue as plain spikes about 7ins. above the cresting. The angle standards are 2ins. by 2ins., set diagonally, with buttresses to each side running from moulded bases and finishing with weatherings under the cresting, above which the standards continue for 12ins. and are crowned by battlemented caps.

The richly crocketed standard to the rails round the Fitzalan tomb in Arundel Chapel,

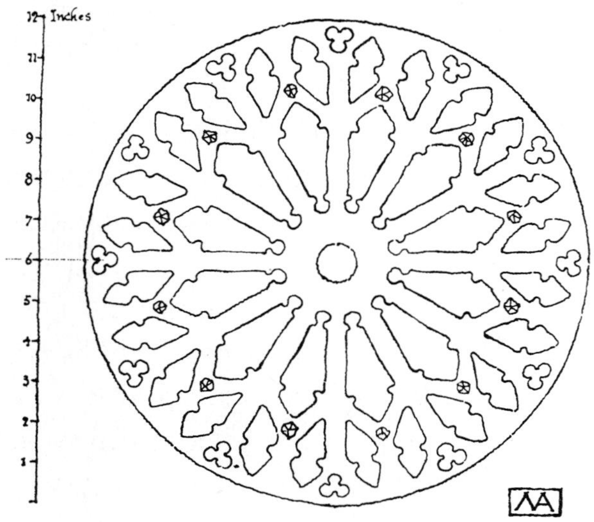

43.—DOOR PLATE FROM S.-W. PORCH, ST. NICHOLAS CHURCH, KENT.

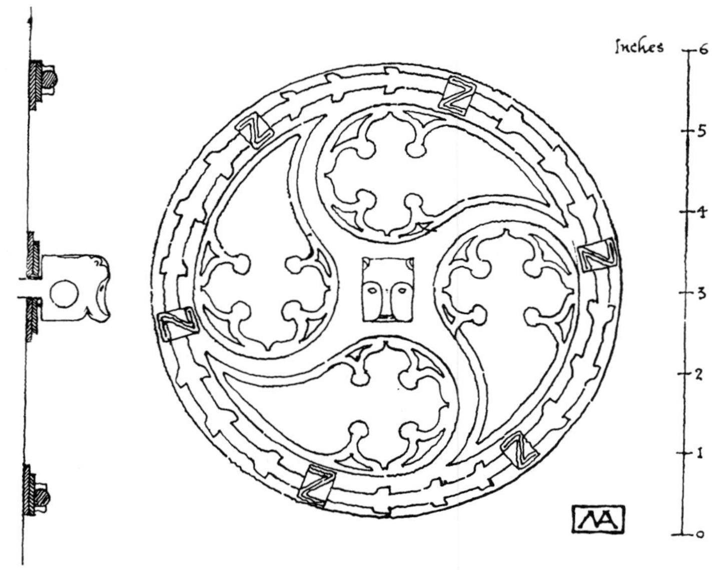

44.—DOOR PLATE FROM THE BEAUCHAMP CHAPEL, ST. MARY'S, WARWICK.

with its cap and pricket for a candle, is a delightful piece of work, which, together with the top rail, was, evidently, largely wrought while hot. The date of the rail is probably 1415.

An interesting screen of a much later date shows that the character remained very much the same up to the sixteenth century. This originally guarded the Urswick Chantry in St. George's Chapel, Windsor, at the north-west corner of the nave, and was described by Sir St. John Hope as follows:

> The foundation in April 1507 by the Dean and Chapter of a chantry in commemoration of Dan Christopher Urswick, sometime Dean, is of interest as giving the dedication of the chapel to which it was attached. . . . Its identity is fixed by the stone and iron enterclose to it with Urswick's arms, etc., which was removed in 1824 to the south aisle of the choir.—(*Windsor Castle*, Vol. II, page 385.)

And later

> It consists of a stone base of four bays 3 ft. 1 in. high. . . . From the top of the stone base rises a tall grate of square iron bars divided by buttresses into four bays with a wider bay continued over the doorway. Each buttress has at the top a shield of the Urswick arms, and the screen is surmounted by a trefoiled cresting with elaborate spiking along the top. The total height is 6 ft. 3 ins.—(*Ibid.*, Vol. II, page 416.)

The most interesting point in the screen is the unusual combination of iron and stone in the design, the one running into the other without the slightest change in the treatment or detail. In Ewelm Church, Oxon, the oaken choir screen has iron instead of wood shafts, but there the moulded bases and caps are of wood, with the iron running through them.

A more typical and altogether charming branch of the fifteenth century smiths' work was the assimilation of the art of the locksmith and the consequent attention given by them to lock cases, door handles and plates. Examples of simple plates to door handles are to be found all over the country. They are usually circular, from 3ins. to 5ins. diameter, cut out of a plain piece of plate iron about one-sixteenth of an inch thick, pierced into tracery patterns, the outer edge being very frequently serrated. Unfortunately, the original drop handles are less common, due to their liability to rust away at the spindle, where they do not come into contact with the hand; for the natural greasing and polishing by hands is, for iron, a certain preservative from corrosion. In the Windsor accounts there are constant items for "white," or tinned, handles and nails, and it is, no doubt, largely due to this process having been in common use for smaller articles that so many still exist.

The porch door to the parish church at St. Nicholas, Kent, has a fine perforated handle plate of unusually large size, being 12ins. in diameter! (Fig. 43.) Its average thickness is one-sixteenth of an inch, but it has the appearance of gradually thinning from the centre outwards, a refinement easily accomplished in hammering out the sheet before piercing, and one which adds very considerably to the beauty of the plate. The original handle is, unfortunately, missing.

More elaborate, though not necessarily of a later date, is the set of three beautiful handle plates in the Beauchamp Chapel at the Church of St. Mary's, Warwick (Figs. 45 and 46). Two are on the doors to the small chantries on the north side of the chapel, both of them have lost their handles, which were probably the same as that to the door on the north side of the altar in the chapel, leading to the library. This is a perfectly plain ring-handle, of $\frac{1}{4}$in. round iron, $2\frac{1}{8}$ins. in diameter inside. The spindle heads to all three plates remain and are all alike. They are delightfully forged conventional bears' heads, representing the crest of the Beauchamp or Nevill family, which is a bear with a ragged staff. The staff is also represented round the outer edge of the plate to the library door, riveted on to the double plates forming the tracery of the plate, which is, in this case, secured to the door by six square bolt heads with the letter "N" (for Nevill) chased upon them. The frame or edge of the two other plates is formed of a delightful reversed battlement or billet moulding and has an exceedingly rich effect. With the exception of the spindle heads, which, as already mentioned, were forged hot, the whole of the work to the plates was cut out of cold iron.

For door fittings of a still more elaborate nature—in fact, examples unique in their richness and dexterity of workmanship—one must return once more to St. George's Chapel, Windsor, where, on one door alone, are three separate pieces unrivalled in Europe. As Sir St. John Hope points out, they are undoubtedly the work of that great smith, John Tresilian, who will be referred to later in describing his masterpiece. It is quite conceivable that he may have made the plates

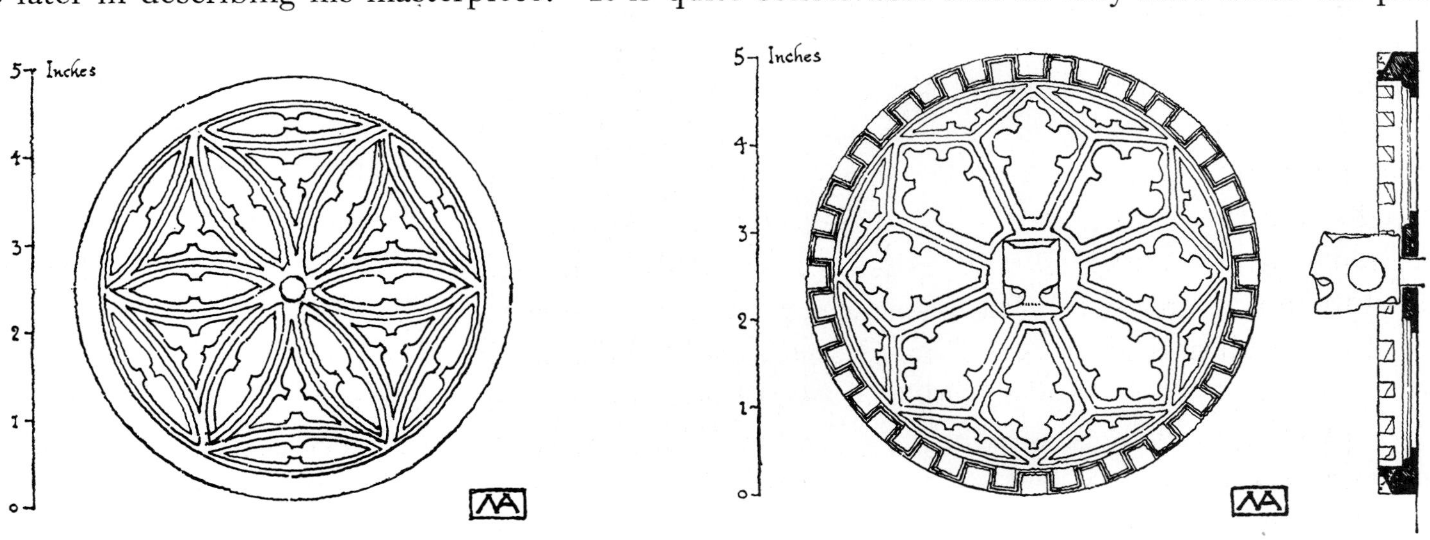

45 AND 46.—DOOR PLATES FROM THE BEAUCHAMP CHAPEL, ST. MARY'S, WARWICK.

in the Beauchamp Chapel also, or, at least, that they were inspired by those on the vice-door at Windsor (Fig. 47). At this time Bishop Beauchamp was acting as surveyor in charge of the works at St. George's Chapel, and it is in his first accounts, from January 11th, 1477 to January 11th, 1478, that we find items referring to the employment of Tresilian. The handle plate is an exquisite piece of work both in design and workmanship, the modelling of the end of the "garter" where it is knotted and falls over being particularly good. The small pierced oriel, closed by a door on the inner side, was probably made for the purposes of confession, and is not only very beautiful, but is also believed to be unique in England. The square lock plate is filled with a diaper design of nine four-petalled flowers, each petal being pierced and cusped. It is curious that, both in this plate and in the very fine one to the door in the screen on the north side of the south choir aisle, the keyhole is clumsily put in without regard to the delicate design of the plates. It will be seen that the diaper in each plate is the same.

47.—VICE-DOOR TO SOUTH CHOIR AISLE, ST. GEORGE'S CHAPEL, WINDSOR.

The "cable" frame and divisions to the larger lock have a small punched enrichment on the face of the spirals reminiscent of earlier work. It is interesting to see how the heads to the rivets or bolts at the four corners securing the lock to the door have been chased after the lock was fixed, to avoid a break in the continuity of the rope pattern.

That St. George's Chapel is rich in examples of smithcraft we have already seen, but there are yet two more pieces, both unique, and both, in all probability, the work of Tresilian. More nearly connected of the two with the door furniture described above is the iron box for offerings, which stands inside the south doorway. The box is octagonal, 17ins. high and 13½ins. wide, and rests upon four circular shafts with hexagonal caps and bases, connected together by a cruciform floor plate. The total height is 3ft. 10½ins. At each angle of the box is a slender buttress running to the top, at the first weathering of which spring ogee crocketed arches over each side or panel, framing the large initial letter "H." The top of the box is flat and has four keyholes with sliding covers alternating with four small castles surrounding a large centre castle. The latter is surmounted by a Royal crown. In the sides of the castle are slits for the insertion of coins, and there are, again, four slits in the cap enclosed by the arches of the crown. There is, unfortunately, no record to show who was the smith who made it or the date when it was made, but there can be little doubt that it was made at the end of the fifteenth century by John Tresilian.

48.—LOCK ON SOUTH DOOR, PRESBYTERY, ST. GEORGE'S CHAPEL, WINDSOR.

Sir St. John Hope gives an interesting bill from the chapter muniments for a similar box, but it is without date or signature :

> " ffor makynge off llj hoops for a Box for Maist' John Shorn the price of the pece—lj. s. sm^{a} (vjs altered to) llj. s
> And for llj lokes to the said Box wt the keys & wt the hed of the box & the key holes kev'ed wt lllj plates to shvtt a pone i ev'quart of the Box wt Xlj Ryvettes to revet the plattes & the hoops to gedd^{r} wt a botom plate the prys of thys psell—sm^{a} .. .. xxs
> sm^{a} to^{llis} (XXVj. s altered to) .. .. XXllj. s."
>
> N.B.—The alterations in the amounts are not by the same hand as the bill.—(*Windsor Castle*, Vol. II, page 459.)

The bill is of value, however, in another direction, as he points out :

> One thing is quite clear, as may be tested by comparing their details, that whoever designed this box also designed the magnificent gates belonging to King Edward IV's tomb, and it is most provoking that no name or date is appended to the bill. It may at any rate be taken for granted that the work was in all probability executed at Windsor, and so furnishes another proof that the box and gates are English, like the writer of the bill.

Edward IV died on April 9th, 1483, and during the last few years of his reign was occupied in building St. George's Chapel and in the preparation of his own tomb and chantry, the gates of which manifest, as did the Eleanor grille at the end of the thirteenth century, the culminating effort of smithcraft of the fifteenth century. So magnificent and impressive in its elaboration is this piece of work that, as one stands before it, it is difficult to realise that it is indeed wrought and cut and constructed out of iron.

First, of its maker: Bishop Beauchamp was appointed surveyor to the Castle February 19th, 1472–73, and his deputy, Thomas Canceller, was appointed "for life" on March 1st, 1476–77. Sir St. John Hope mentions that the earliest surviving account of Bishop Beauchamp for the year 1478 is headed by conditions and payment of various people, mentioning a master smith (together with a master carpenter and a master carver) as having ten shillings a year for his gowns (*Ibid.*, Vol. II, page 377).

49.—ALMS BOX, ST. GEORGE'S CHAPEL, WINDSOR.

In 1479, among the receipts is one for £20 6s. 8d.:

> Expenses of John Tresilian, the chief smith, at London looking after the making of a great anvil for six days and for the carriage of the same to Windsor.—(*Ibid.*, Vol. II, page 378.)

And under an account of wages paid:

> To John Tresilian, head smith, at 16d. a day .. .. £23-5/-.
> —(*Ibid.*, Vol. II, page 378.)

And a further item:

> and for making of a mill for the use of the smiths, and a house for the masons working upon the tomb of the lord King, and a chimney within the same.—(*Ibid.*, Vol. II, page 381.)

So high a wage as 16d. per day is sufficient to show that Tresilian was a master smith of very special ability, and the fact that he was retained as the master smith at Windsor during the time that the smiths were "working upon the tomb of the lord King" is sufficient evidence that he was the maker of it, in spite of the statement made by Mr. Willsment, and repeated by others, that it was the work of Quentin Matsys of Louvain.

As Sir St. John Hope points out, since Matsys—

> was not born until 1466 and the iron gates under notice were probably made just before the death of Edward IV in 1483, it is quite impossible that they can be his work.—(*Ibid.*, Vol. II, page 428.)

The gates are, unfortunately, not standing in their original position, having been removed in 1789 to the presbytery, where they now are. Sir St. John Hope describes their original

50.—GATES AND SCREEN TO CHANTRY OF EDWARD IV, ST. GEORGE'S CHAPEL, WINDSOR.

51.—LOCK TO CHOIR DOOR, ST. GEORGE'S CHAPEL, WINDSOR.

position as having been probably—

> across the aisle, just west of the King's grave. . . . It was evidently King Edward's intention that these first two bays of the aisle proper should form his chapel or "enclosure." There was probably a screen of some kind across the aisle to the East of his tomb (with a doorway in it for processions) and the pair of iron gates stood West of it.—(*Ibid.*)

The width of the screen, including the side towers, is 11ft. 6ins., the double gates being 6ft. 6ins. wide and the towers each 2ft. 6ins. wide, and 9ft. high. The height of the gates is 5ft. 4ins. The illustrations are the best and fullest description that can be given, and it is, therefore, scarcely necessary to do more than call attention to a few of the main points.

The two gates are constructed of four main vertical bars and a top and bottom rail to which are riveted the ornamental buttresses and the intermediate tracery, the whole of which is constructed in the manner employed in Henry V's chantry at Westminster Abbey, already described, the work in this instance, however, being infinitely more elaborate and complicated. The towers are built up in the same way upon an internal frame—

> the top of which has an inner series of holes suggestive of some further upper member, such as a pinnacle or dome incompleted or lost.

52.—LOCK FROM THE ROYAL FEMALE ORPHAN ASYLUM (PREVIOUSLY BEDDINGTON HALL). (*Victoria and Albert Museum.*)

An examination of the detail illustration shows that the first band of tracery above the plinth is a series of squares filled with the same four-petalled flower with cusped piercings as was used in the diaper of the lock plates, and it is again used in a band round the towers at a level with the top of the gates. In the pierced band or cresting to the gates is the same detail as the open-work front to the oriel in the vice-door. It will be noticed that the design of the gates is carried round the towers up to the band of flower tracery already mentioned, above which the tracery changes.

This screen, perhaps more than any other piece of fifteenth century ironwork, has been variously described, in a derogatory sense, as "*joiners'* or *carpenters'*" work, meaning that its construction as well as its design are not that proper to the use of the smith. This has already been referred to, but the criticism is so unreasonable that no excuse is made for returning to it. So far as the design is concerned, no objections are raised to the oak stalls to the choir at St. George's (made at the same time) on the ground that they represent a stone design reproduced in wood; and, as regards construction, an examination of any wood screen of this period will reveal a clumsiness and crudity of handling far removed from the ingenious fitting together displayed by the smith. At this time, woodwork was, wherever possible, cut out of the solid, building up and "planting on" being rarely resorted to; while "masons'" joints were more commonly used than mitres, as none of the elaborate methods for framing and building up woodwork, now employed by joiners and cabinet-makers, was then known. The only resemblances to woodwork, therefore, were that the iron was sawn and carved when cold, and joints were made by means of halving, tenoning, rebating and pinning, none of which should be regarded as a matter of reproach to the smith.

53.—HERSE, SWARFORD CHURCH, LINCS.

To return to the monument once more. We know from early records that it was originally completely gilded. Sandford writes:

> a Monument of Steel polish'd and gilt, representing a Pair of Gates between Two Towers, all of curious transparent Workmanship after the *Gothic* Manner.

and Ashmole describes them as—

> a range of Steel gilt, set to inclose it from the North Isle, cut excellently well in Churchwork.

It is now entirely black and is, probably, finer so. As Sir St. John Hope remarks, it is regrettable that it should be in its present position, where the gates are practically unopenable and are obviously useless.

The fifteenth century, like the thirteenth century, thus comes to an end with a triumphant effort, and wrought iron once again ceases to be used for decorative purposes. The introduction of Italian workmen skilled in the art of casting in bronze was probably the greatest factor in causing this decline in smithcraft. Henry VII may well have felt that the magnificence of Edward's tomb could neither be excelled in iron nor, perhaps, equalled, and turned to Torrigiano to produce for him in bronze a monument which would be regarded as an advance upon that of his predecessor. Others followed his example; Thomas Waley, Archbishop of York, whose tomb was taken at his death and altered for Henry VIII; the gilt bronze guard-rail or screen to the tomb of Charles, Earl of Worcester, and his wife, in St. George's Chapel, and many others.

The sixteenth century is as barren as the fourteenth, and there are only a few and, for the most part, unimportant examples left to show that what little was done by the smiths was influenced, as always, by the changes in the architecture of the day.

Ely Cathedral presents two interesting examples of chantry gates: firstly, those to Bishop Alcock's Chapel, date 1488; and, secondly, and of greater interest, the gate and screen to Bishop West's Chapel of 1538.

Mr. Starkie Gardner says:

> Tradition has assigned them to Quentin Matsys, *and there can be no doubt as to their Flemish origin.* . . . The design forms an upper tier of linear panels of twisted bars, with forged caps and bases, and very richly traceried arches; and a more severe lower tier of narrower panels, with a base of pierced tracery, a band of very Flemish arabesque work and a top of very beautiful traceried arches, including fleurs-de-lis and shields. Above all this panel work are some heavy branching interlaced scrolls filling in the arch, and exactly recalling the work of the Antwerp well cover, except that they blossom into Tudor roses instead of leaves. A touch of Flemish Renaissance feeling is given by the massive turned and moulded slam-bar.—(*Ironwork*, page 122.)

So definite a statement, coming from this source, should not be lightly challenged, but it seems hardly fair to ascribe to foreigners any English work, save where there is stronger evidence than a close resemblance to Continental work. It was at one time the opinion of many that the finely stamped work of the end of the thirteenth century was French—indeed, even now one is told at Chester that the ironwork on the aumbry doors was made in Liége! Luckily, the accounts for the Eleanor grille are irrefutable proof that there were English smiths capable of producing this work. The records already quoted of John Tresilian, though not so complete, are sufficient, and as we proceed farther it will be seen that one of the most praiseworthy characteristics of the English smiths was their remarkable receptiveness combined with an individuality which was never lost. Until further evidence is forthcoming, therefore, it would be fairer to describe the West screen as at least of doubtful origin.

A lock of great interest (Fig. 52) has recently found, in the Victoria and Albert Museum, a resting place of greater security than that which it had in the hands of the guardians of the Royal Female Orphan Asylum at Beddington. Beddington Hall was built by Sir Francis Carew, the son of Sir Nicholas Carew, who held high office under Henry VIII. A member of the committee of management of the orphanage wrote to the Press that the lock was for sale—

> and that while the Committee would infinitely prefer that, as an act of generosity by some patriotic donor it should find a place in the London Museum, *they are not prepared to refuse the money of any bona fide purchaser be he English or American.*

As will be seen, it bears the Royal arms upon a sliding shutter which conceals the keyhole, and which is liberated by moving the small knob above it, the knob being formed to resemble a man's head.

Even in the sixteenth century St. George's Chapel is again able to furnish an example, in the shape of a charming Jacobean lock, in which pierced plate iron is seen to lend itself admirably to the simple " strap " ornament of the period. The " cable " or " rope " framing the lock is carelessly worked, with no attempt to finish properly at the corners. This twisted rope or cable is one of the commonest forms of enrichment in ironwork up to the end of the seventeenth century, probably on account of the ease with which an effect can be produced in this way. In this case it has been carved out of the cold iron; but where it is used in heavier work it meant simply the twisting of a bar of iron of any section while hot.

54.—DOOR, ST. SAVIOUR'S, DARTMOUTH.

A good example of the varied use of the cable pattern is found in the guard-rail to the Lincoln Chapel, St. George's, Windsor " originally known as that of Master John Shorne." Its date is 1584. On the top rail small cable mouldings form the top and bottom members, which run in opposite directions to one another, and the top bar of the gate is similarly enriched with a somewhat larger rope. The main standards are an interesting variation of the plain twisted square bar, for grooves have been cut down the centre of the sides further to enrich them. A variety of sections was used in the same way, each obtaining entirely different effects, such as a flat bar with square arrises or with the arrises rounded.

The great fleurs-de-lys terminals finishing with acorn tops are full of character, and their similarity to those of the grille from Snarford Church, Lincolnshire (now in the Victoria and

55.—SOUTH-WEST GATE, CANTERBURY CATHEDRAL.

Albert Museum), is worthy of notice. The latter is labelled as being of the fifteenth century, but, in the absence of any actual evidence of this date being correct, it would seem wisest to place it in the latter part of the sixteenth or the beginning of the seventeenth century. The very free form of the flowers or plumes on either side of the central lily are certainly more in keeping with the later date. While it is not uncommon to find smiths still using forms of the century preceding their own, the grille at Snarford would, if a fifteenth century example, be a very extraordinary instance of premonition in design.

It is difficult to estimate how far the growing feeling against the manufacture of iron in England during the sixteenth century affected the use of it for decorative purposes.

Alarmed by the enormous consumption of timber necessary for the process of its manufacture and the consequent deforestation of the country in the localities where iron ore was abundant, the Government passed no fewer than three Acts of Parliament during the reign of Queen Elizabeth, for the preservation of timber and the prohibition of the further increase of ironworks.

Indeed, Mr. J. B. Waring points out that, so far back as the thirteenth century Henry III revoked a grant given to the Cistercian Abbey at Haxley in Gloucestershire by Henry II for—

> an iron forge in the Forest of Dean and two oaks weekly to supply it with fuel.—(*Masterpieces of Industrial Art and Sculpture, International Exhibition*, 1862.)

—on the ground that it was prejudicial to the forest. The same writer refers to records of seventy-two furnaces for "melting iron ore" having been built in the Forest of Dean during the reign of Edward I. The Sussex Archæological Society's *Transactions* refer to nearly a hundred sites of extinct smelting furnaces, and—

> Camden writing in the year 1586 speaks of the country being full of iron mines and furnaces.—(*Ibid.*)

In view of the fact that a large supply of timber was then of the first importance to the country both for ship and other building, and that oak, the best timber for these purposes, was also the best for the manufacture of iron, it is not surprising, the ironworks having become so numerous, that the manufacture should have been first regarded with dislike, and then discouraged. The great increase in the number of ironworks was, no doubt, largely due to an Act, passed in 1354, referred to by Mr. John Nicholls, preventing the exportation of iron from England, which, he adds, was insufficient for the growing prosperity of the country. Furthermore, he says:

England was at this time principally supplied with iron and steel from Spain and Germany, and the foreign merchants of the Steel-yard enjoyed the chief advantages of this trade.

While only a small proportion of the iron made was used at any period for the purposes dealt with in the preceding pages, any repression of its manufacture would have the effect of reducing that proportion, if only from the necessarily increased cost of the material. Generally speaking, however, it will have been seen that decorative ironwork flourished during times of peace, and vanished to an extraordinary degree (compared with other crafts attendant on architecture) during periods of war and unrest, for the smiths were at such times immediately recalled to the sterner branch of their trade.

We have seen the fortunes of smithcraft rise, fall and rise again, only to fall once more for a still longer period of inactivity, lasting, indeed, until the gradual awakening in the seventeenth century. It was this awakening and endeavour which fitted the English smiths for the sudden rise in their fortunes which awaited them in 1689, with the arrival of their greatest patrons, William and Mary.

55A.—PADLOCK FROM MORPETH CITY GAOL. SIXTEENTH CENTURY.
(Victoria and Albert Museum.)

CHAPTER IV

SEVENTEENTH CENTURY DEVELOPMENTS

THE iron industry had reached such dimensions at the end of the sixteenth century as to arouse considerable alarm, by reason of the enormous amount of timber required to feed the furnaces which now abounded all over the country. The Acts passed during the reign of Queen Elizabeth instituting heavy fines on all new iron-works had the immediate effect of stimulating the inventive faculties of those concerned in the manufacture, and as early as 1589 a Mr. Proctor attempted to convert iron ore with pit-coal instead of charcoal. In 1612 and 1613 patents were granted to Simon Stentarent and John Ravenson, respectively, for processes of manufacture by coal, but these and others all ended in failure, until, in 1619, Dud Dudley, a natural son of Edward, Lord Dudley, succeeded.

56.—EARLY EXAMPLE OF OVERTHROW, DOUBLE GATES AND SIDE PANELS TO CHAPEL, BREDON CHURCH.

The story of his life, gleaned from

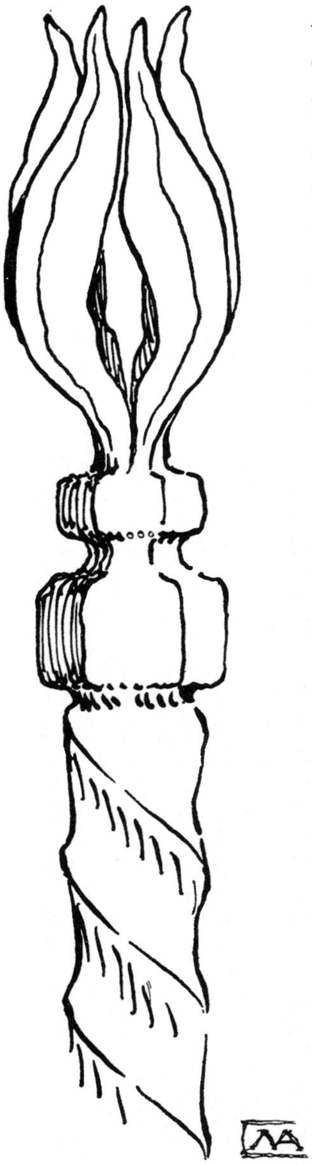

Metallum Martis, practically an autobiography, is dramatic in its revelation of a man harried and hampered on all sides and eventually crushed. Few men, happily, are called upon to undergo so severe a trial of their strength and energy before finally being compelled to acknowledge defeat. Born in the year 1599, he was at Balliol College, Oxford, when his father sent for him in 1619 to take charge of his iron-works, consisting of one blast furnace and two forges at Pensnett, Worcestershire. He at once directed his attention to the possibilities of using pit-coal in place of charcoal, altering his furnace to the requirements of the new process. His success was immediate and the quality of the iron good, though " the quantity did not exceed above 3 tons per week."

Lord Dudley applied for a patent, which was granted for thirty-one years, and a year later, at the King's command, a quantity of the new iron was sent up to London, where it was tested at the Tower and found to be good and merchantable. But the vested interests in the manufacture of iron by means of charcoal were enormous. Dudley writes:

57.—STANDARDS TO RETURN WINGS, BURLEIGH HOUSE, STAMFORD.

> More cheaper iron there cannot be made, for the author did sell pig of cast iron, made with pit-cole at four pounds per tun, many tuns in the twentieth year of King James (1623), with good profit ; of late charcole pig iron hath been sold at six pounds per tun, yea at seven pounds per tun hath much been sold. Also the Author did sell bar iron good and merchantable at twelve pounds per tun and under, but since bar iron hath been sold for the most part Ever since at £15, £16, £17 and £18 per tun by charcole iron masters.

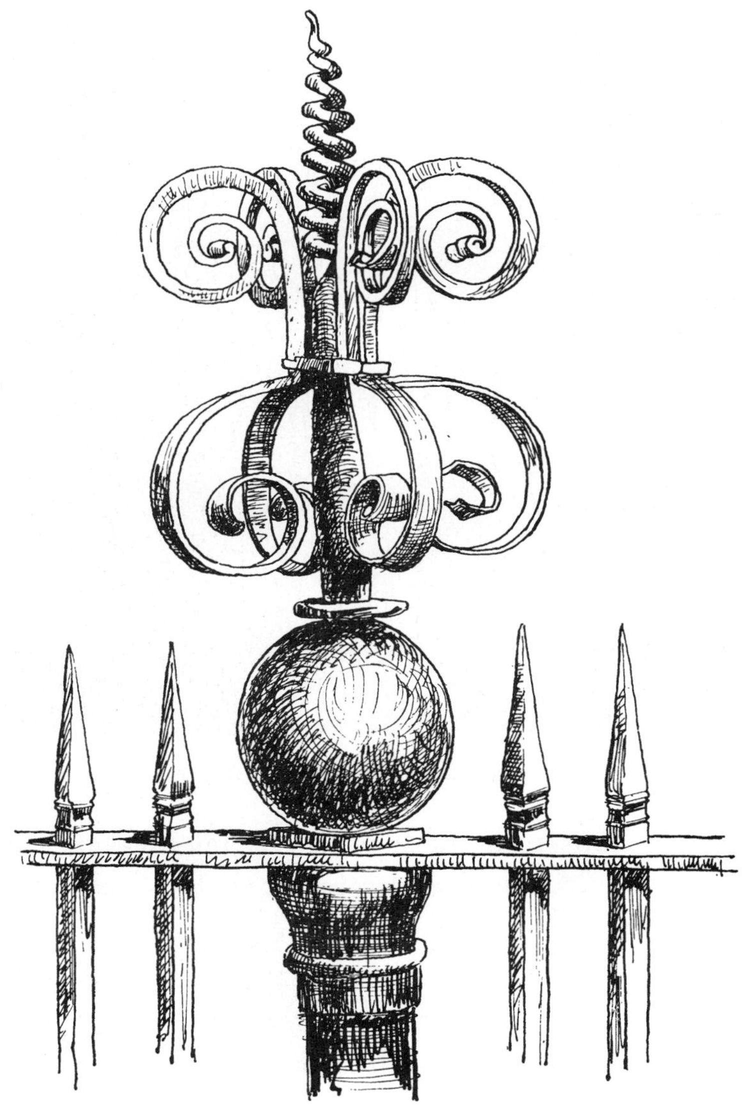

58.—DETAIL, WARBURTON CHAPEL SCREEN, ST. JOHN'S CHURCH, CHESTER.

The latter were quick to see the danger of his success to their own market and, recognising the magnitude of his invention and the revolution it must cause in the iron world if allowed to grow, they immediately combined together with the one purpose of crushing him by any means in their power.

The production of iron by charcoal necessarily entailed the employment of a vast number of people in felling, carting timber and charcoal burning (Yarranton, in 1677, speaks of sixty thousand people being employed in the iron trade in the Forest of Dean alone). It was, therefore, an easy matter for the ironmasters to inflame the minds of these workers, on the ground that Dudley's success spelt ruin and starvation to them, with the result that on several occasions they rose in a body and destroyed his works. As though this were not sufficient, Nature also stepped in and swept away his works at Cradley by flood! Ultimately, the masters were successful in

59.—WARBURTON CHAPEL SCREEN, ST. JOHN'S CHURCH, CHESTER.

ousting him from these works altogether and, following him relentlessly, they involved him in law suits, circulated evil reports of his iron, and even petitioned the King to put a stop "to the dangerous innovation of smelting iron with coal," insisting that, if allowed to continue, it must inevitably result in "some great public calamity."

With wonderful energy and spirit he continued in spite of all discouragement, and established other works at Hindley and Hascobridge, where, he says, with a furnace all of stone, 27 feet square and fitted with unusually large bellows, he was able, when at full work, to produce seven tons a week. The fight was too unequal, however, and he eventually succumbed, became a soldier, was taken prisoner, escaped to Bristol and ultimately died in Worcestershire in 1684 at the age of eighty-five, without disclosing his secret.

It was not until 1713 that the use of pit-coal was again successfully attempted, and probably about 1757 before it came into general use, thus more than a century was lost! In *An Account of the Iron Works in the Forest of Dean*, by Henry Powles, dated 1677–78, he says:

Several attempts have been made to bring in the use of Sea-coal in these Works, instead of Charcoal; the former being to be had at an easie rate, the latter not without great expense, but hitherto they have proved ineffectual. The Workmen finding by experience, that a Sea-coal Fire, how vehement so ever, will not penetrate the most fixed parts of the Ore, and so leaveth much of the Metal unmelted.

The "account" is of so much interest, in giving a detailed description of the production of iron at this time and the manner in which it was prepared for sale to the smiths, that it has

60.—WARBURTON CHAPEL SCREEN, ST. JOHN'S CHURCH, CHESTER (DETAILS).

been given in full in Appendix II, together with quotations from a spirited pamphlet, published the same year by "Andrew Yarranton, Gent, London," bearing the amusing title "England's Improvements by Sea and Land to Out-do the Dutch without Fighting, to Pay Debts without Moneys," written in defence of iron manufacture and an argument against its suppression, which was still actively discussed by many. (See Appendix III.)

Powles' account is of particular interest in that it shows that at this time the ironmasters supplied the smiths with "Bars of several shapes and sizes." How long this had been the custom is not definitely known, but it is clear from this that the smiths, of the seventeenth century at least, were saved the preliminary labour of beating out the "blooms" or rough lumps of iron (already referred to in the Introduction) supplied to them in the early times. These bars were, no doubt, of a very rough description, but the fact that they were of various sizes must have effected an enormous saving of labour in the output of the gates, railings, etc., which, we shall

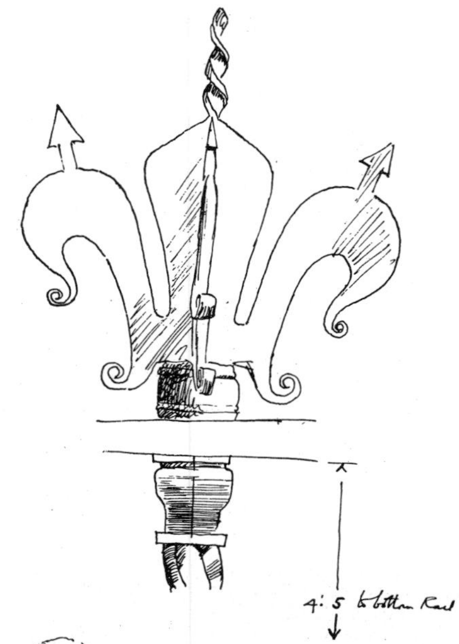

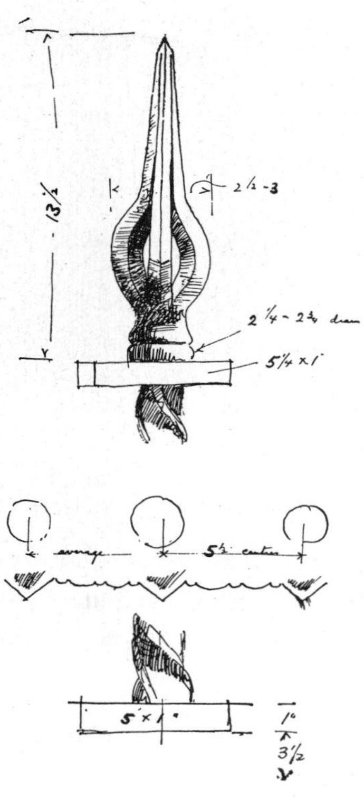

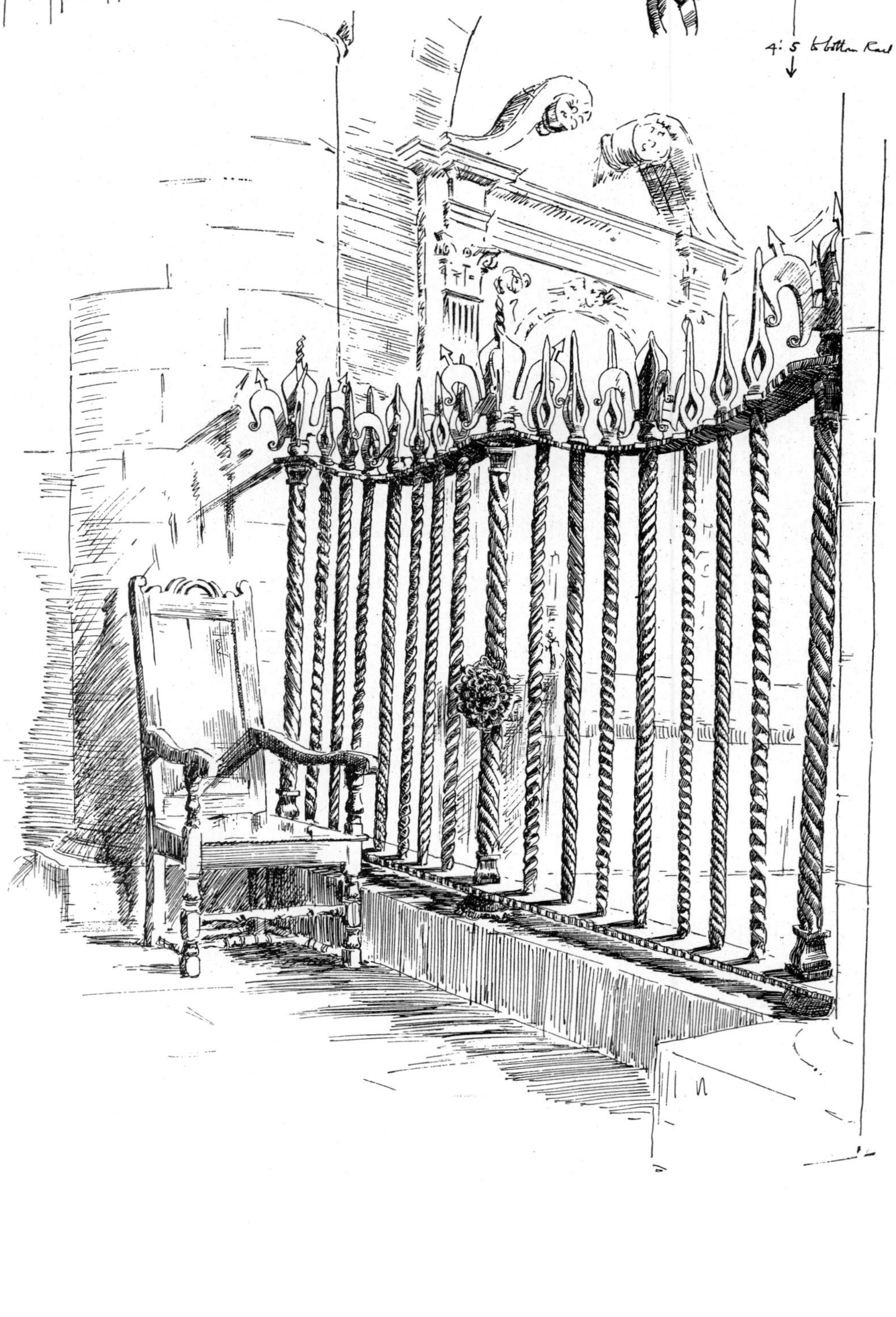

61.—WARBURTON CHAPEL SCREEN, ST. JOHN'S CHURCH, CHESTER.

see, were made in such numbers all over the country during the last years of the seventeenth century and the first half of the eighteenth century.

It is a matter for regret that it was long before the English architects of the seventeenth century saw an opening for the use of decorative ironwork in the architecture of the Renaissance, and we are thus left with but few examples to guide us, although many pieces, no doubt, were destroyed or the iron used for re-forging.

The gates and railings at Cowdray House are of the greatest value in that they furnish a very strong connecting link between the tomb rails of the fifteenth century and the garden gates

62.—GROOMBRIDGE PLACE, KENT. LATE SEVENTEENTH CENTURY.
Iron bars in a wooden framing, and a cresting of spikes and fleurs-de-lys, such as preceded gates made all of iron.

and railings of the end of the seventeenth century. From the fact, however, that they are the sole remaining example of this type, it may be concluded that they were unusual at the time they were probably made, that is, the end of the sixteenth or the first years of the seventeenth century. It was not until towards the end of the seventeenth century that large open iron gates and palisades gradually came into fashion, creating the main outlet for the industry of the smiths of the future and affording an opening for serious architectural design in wrought ironwork.

63.—GATES FACING RIVER, HAM HOUSE.

64.—WOODEN GATES WITH IRON BARS, OF EARLY TYPE, AT HUTTON-IN-THE-FOREST, CUMBERLAND.

To return to the Cowdray gates (taking first the features which are distinctly of fifteenth century character), the main standards are square below, buttressed on all four sides and, rising from a chamfered base, become spirally twisted above ; the 4in. deep rail cutting the standards has the cable mould at top and bottom, and the flat plate sides decorated with crest and rose alternately ; the edges of the horizontal bars to the railings are cabled and the vertical bars are set diagonally, and finish alternately in spikes and fleurs-de-lys. The premonition of the

65.—SIDE GATES, HAM HOUSE.

Renaissance is seen in the buttresses to the standards, which, in place of the weathered representations of stonework, are cut in shapes reminiscent of the shaped wooden slat balusters frequently found in Elizabethan staircases. Intermediate dog bars with flat arrow heads, though still twisted, are an innovation, and the use of single C scrolls between the bars makes its appearance.

That magnificent Elizabethan mansion, Burleigh House, Stamford, may have possessed similar gates and railings, for the standards to the eighteenth century gates to the forecourt are strengthened from behind by being connected up to single standards evidently of an earlier date and, possibly, relics of original Elizabethan gates. They are single upright bars, one on each side, of $1\frac{1}{4}$in. square bar twisted and finished in an octagonal, pomegranate-shaped cap, with a large open tulip flower springing from it (Fig. 57).

66.—GATES TO AVENUE, HAM HOUSE.

The double gates and side panels of plain stout square bars enclosing the Side Chapel in Bredon Church are a fine straightforward piece of work. The acorn-like ends to the dog-bars are unusual, and so are the two-tier spikes above the top bar, which, in this case, is carried right across free of the gates. It will be seen later how vitally important a feature of all gates this connecting bar became (Fig. 56).

The first indication of the coming change from wholly wooden gates is found in the introduction of open panels filled with iron bars or turned wooden balusters, the dipping towards the centre in an inverted arch of the top rail and the addition of iron crestings of spikes in various forms along the top. The gates to the Warburton Chapel in St. John's Church, Chester, afford a fine example. Two other examples are illustrated. The first is at Groombridge Place, Kent, where are late

67.—GATES TO AVENUE, HAM HOUSE.

seventeenth century gates of iron bars in a wooden framing, and a cresting of spikes and fleurs-de-lys. Here the finely proportioned gate-piers were evidently inspired, if not designed, by Wren, and the niches have been unusually placed to face each other instead of, in the usual manner, to face the road (Fig. 62). The second, and less important example, comes from Hutton-in-the-Forest, Cumberland.

68.—STAIRCASE BALUSTRADE, CRAIGIEHALL.

The wooden gate died hard, and one finds eventually only the wooden frame retained and the remainder entirely formed of iron bars. In the great gates to Ham House this type is imitated on a large scale but totally constructed of iron. (Fig. 63). These gates are not, as Mr. Starkie Gardner suggests, of the same date as the house, namely, about 1610, but were made for Lady Dysart in Scotland in 1671, under the supervision of her architect, Sir William Bruce. The authority for this can be found in Mylne's *Master Masons to the Crown of Scotland*, on page 167, and elsewhere. The side gates and the great gate to the avenue and Ham Common are equally interesting (Figs. 65 and 66). The side gates and screen are of pleasing proportions, and are plain without being dull. The simple overthrow carries some well modelled tulips, and the treatment of these flowers and the twisted spikes and scrolls of the middle bar is reminiscent of, though more refined than, similar details in the gates at Traquair Castle, which are described later.

The gates facing Ham Common are more imposing, but hardly more pleasing. Their scale is enormous, and the clumsy branched spikes on the overthrow add to their forbidding air. This overthrow is important, for it shows an early attempt to combine the coat of arms and coronet as an integral part of the design—a feature which was later more successfully treated (Fig. 67).

69.—ROOF CRESTING, GLAMIS CASTLE, FORFARSHIRE.

A very free treatment characterises the work of the smiths up to 1689. It bears little trace of architectural supervision, and reminds one forcibly of the simple crudeness often exhibited in the work of the stonemason and joiner of the sixteenth century. The smith, without architectural training to guide him, turned to naturalistic forms, and large, loosely designed flowers having little or no connection with the main lines are common features, particularly in Scottish ironwork, where the influence which was to alter English work so materially was not felt until later. These flowers (the tulip was a special favourite) are, more often than not, beautifully modelled, and are really fine exhibitions of forging, which have a great charm of their own ; the balustrade to the staircase at Craigiehall is an example of this. The C scrolls of circular iron, filling the panels between the uprights, are clumsy ; on the other hand, the tulip flower in the centre panel could scarcely be more graceful (Fig. 68).

The iron cresting to the roof of Glamis Castle, Forfarshire (Fig. 69), shows a curious combination of flat strapwork and alternate plain, square and twisted standards finishing

70.—TRAQUAIR CASTLE, PEEBLES-SHIRE. ENTRANCE GATES.

in terminals representing the lily, rose and thistle. The date is probably 1687 or a little earlier, as the third Earl of Strathmore was at work upon the castle from 1670 to 1687.

The gates and open palisade to Traquair Castle are notable examples of the transition from the Gothic to the Renaissance. The elaborate overthrow is a new feature still retaining the inverted arch shape of the later wooden gates, at the same time introducing the coronet and coat of arms which formed so important a feature in the later overthrow. The cresting is formed of loose scrolls finishing with roses, and branching from the scrolls, quite regardless of their natural curves, are six large tulips, out of scale with the rest of the work. The space between the two stout horizontal bars which form the base of the overthrow is filled with tight scrolls springing from the lower bar. Each completes two and a half whorls. These are repeated along the bottom bar of the gates between the vertical bars, and have a distinct Gothic flavour. So also have the fleurs-de-lys spikes on the second and top rails, and the trident prickets to the two middle rails with their twisted centre tongue. The flat fleurs-de-lys heads to the alternate bars of the palisade show a desire for new form in the extended side petals and the addition of

71.—ENTRANCE GATES AND PALISADE, TRAQUAIR CASTLE.

the two meaningless antennæ. In short, the work impresses one as having a feeling of uncertainty and craving for a new treatment, without any definite knowledge of how it is to be arrived at.

A very similar treatment of wrought iron is to be seen in the early sword-rests at Bristol. The earliest known example stands in the centre of the nave in St. Philip's and St. Jacob's Church, and it is of particular value, for, as can be seen in Fig. 76, the date 1610 is stamped in very small numerals on the plate-iron enrichment and, so far as we know, this remarkable fact has escaped the notice of previous writers on this subject. It is curious that the first three numerals of the date 1610 are cut through the iron plate with a chisel and the o is merely stamped as a small hole. For such an early date, the treatment is extraordinarily delicate and small,

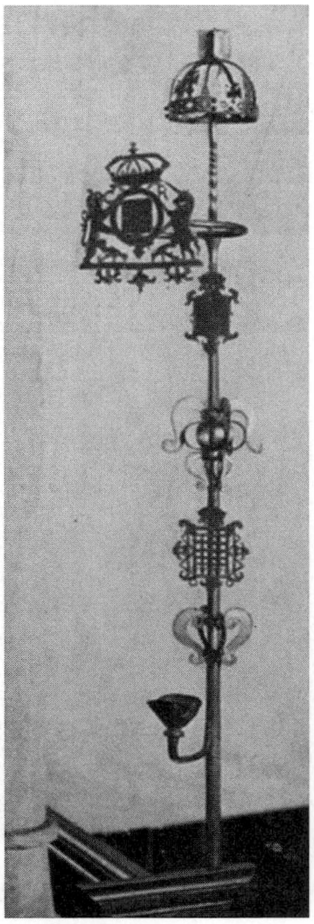

72.—SWORD - REST, ST. AUGUSTINE'S, BRISTOL.

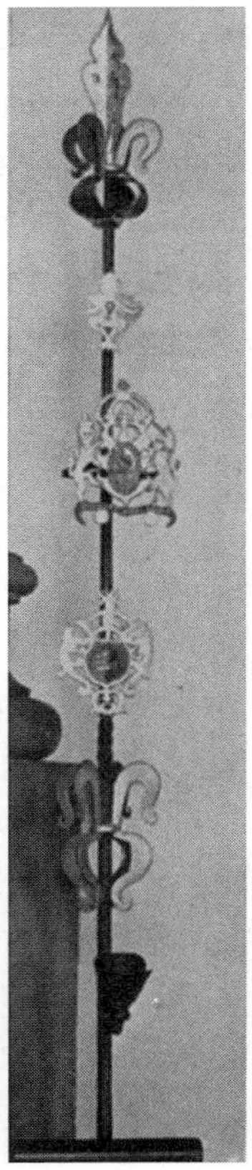

73.—SWORD-REST, ST. MICHAEL'S CHURCH, BRISTOL.

74.—SWORD-REST, ST. MARY-LE-PORT, BRISTOL.

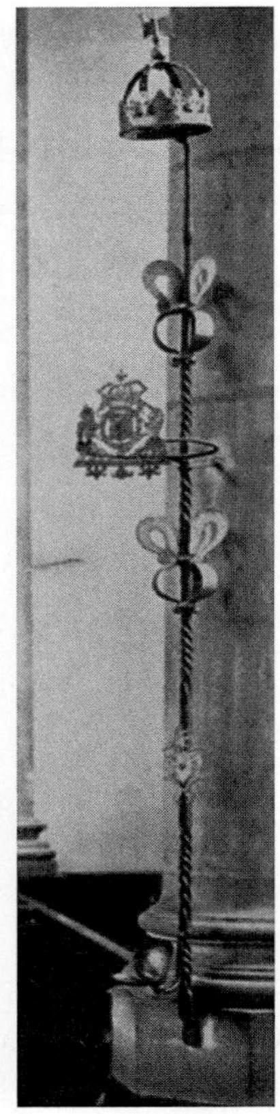

75.—SWORD - REST, CHRIST CHURCH, BRISTOL.

76.—DETAIL OF SWORD-REST ILLUSTRATED BELOW.

77.—CHOIR RAIL, PARISH CHURCH, WREXHAM.

78.—ST. PHILIP'S AND ST. JACOB'S, BRISTOL.

except for the ring, which is large in proportion to the whole. Rivet holes in the standard above this ring seem to indicate that a rest for the blade, possibly sickle-shaped, formed a part of the original design. Above this, again, the standard terminates in a gilded fleur-de-lys instead of the usual crown. At first sight, the two ornamental flowers which enrich the stem appear to be of different design, but upon inspection it will be seen that the smith has accomplished this effect by the ingenious method of giving the square bar between the two flowers a half twist, thus presenting to the eye first the diagonal and then the four-square view of the same flower.

79.—SMALL GATE, MALPAS CHURCH, CHESHIRE.

A very similar early sword-rest can be seen attached to the south pier of the chancel arch in Christ Church, Bristol, while there is a third early sword-rest at the Church of St. Mary-le-Port, which for many years lay forgotten in a cellar, but which is now restored to its rightful place. In this example there are indications, however, of a later date, particularly in the refinement of flattening the scroll ends into modelled leaves. There are also the remains of a pair of beaked grotesques (which one authority describes as a two-headed eagle), strangely out of date with the surmounting crown and the twisted standard, and it may well be that they were added later as the cresting to a shield. They are of embossed thin sheet and have a small hook attached, and, if they had been a feature of the original sword-rest,

80.—PAIR OF GATES, COTE HOUSE, OXON.

the crown surmounting the whole would have been carried out with at least an equal richness. The height from the foot to the apex of the crown is just short of seven feet. The cup from the base of the sword-rest is missing.

Another remarkably fine sword-rest of the early seventeenth century type may be seen in St. Michael's Church, Bristol. This rest is 5ft. 1in. in height, measuring from the pew-end, to which it is fixed, to the top of the fleur-de-lys. The latter is unusually elaborate and of pleasing design, while the cup is of the usual two-petalled sort found in the earlier sword-rests at St. Philip's and St. Jacob's, Christ Church and St. Augustine's.

At St. Augustine's the sword-rest, while it belongs to the early period, shows traces of somewhat later date in its greater elaboration, and especially in the diminution and scrolling of the leaf ends of the flat-plate ornament. This is probably the latest of the seventeenth century examples. From its wood support to the apex of the crown, measured to the top of the Maltese cross, the height is 4ft. 11ins.

81.—CRANE FOR FONT COVER, ST. MICHAEL, QUEENHYTHE.

All the above examples are from Bristol, which is a city particularly rich in this type of wrought iron. There is one more example belonging to the seventeenth century housed in St. John's Church; the remainder date from the eighteenth century, and are described in the next chapter. St. John's Church, picturesquely placed upon the city wall of Bristol, contains two early examples of wrought iron-work. The hour-glass stand, an illustration of which appears on page 69, and an early sword-rest. Of their respective types, the former is one of the finest and largest, and the latter one of the smallest, for it is only 4ft. 6ins. high and 10½ins. wide.

The Parish Church, Wrexham, possesses a unique choir rail, which, though probably of the last years of the seventeenth century or early eighteenth century, combines features characteristic of both, as well as of the fifteenth and sixteenth centuries. Design is practically non-existent, and the general effect, as might be expected, is one of indescribable muddle; and yet it abounds in interest, for it shows a surprising knowledge of many various types of detail. We find the mediæval work represented in the twisted bar, the bar diagonally set and the panel of many whorled scrolls. It is interesting to note the main standards, which are made up of the flat bars placed together and twisted. The smaller twisted standards are of single flat section, and are of a rather unusually quick twist. Again, the acanthus leaves surrounding the cherub mask, and the leaves to the vine which trails over the dipping top rail of the gates are Gothic in feeling, while the mask and the vine (apart from the leaves), the great lily terminal to the gate standard, the flat pomegranates and what is, apparently, an orange tree growing from an urn are all distinctly of the seventeenth century. On the other hand, the sprig of bay or laurel was not in common use until the early eighteenth century, yet here it is combined with the mediæval twisted bar as its main stem. The urn, as ludicrously out of scale with its contents as it is with its surroundings, has a delicacy of treatment which might well be late eighteenth century. Owing

82.—IRON CRESTING TO WOODEN GATES AT HAMPSTEAD MARSHALL.

its interest largely to its failures, it is evidently the work of a receptive brain, quick to seize upon new modes of expression, but hampered in the proper use of them by lack of knowledge. Though there is no documentary evidence of it, the smith who made the rails may, quite possibly, have been Hugh Davies of Groes Foel, Bersham, near Wrexham, who died in 1702, and by his will, dated June 13th of that year, left his " messuage in Bersham with appurtenances " to his wife Eleanor and then to his son Robert, together with a sum of £7 10s., " for which he is to instruct my son Thomas in the trade and science of a smith." It is at least pleasant to think that the

83.—CHANDELIER HANGER, ST. MICHAEL'S CHURCH, QUEENHYTHE.
(*Victoria and Albert Museum.*)

choir rail may have been the work of the father of Robert Davies, and so to explain the source from which the latter received the first inspiration, which later fitted him for the important place he was to take among the smiths of the eighteenth century.

The dignified little gate across the sunk path leading through the churchyard at Malpas, Cheshire, not far from Wrexham, may have been by Hugh Davies also. It is extraordinarily successful in its simplicity. The little dog-bars linked up to the main bars and the graduation of the scrolled cresting are both delightful. Its superiority over the Wrexham choir rail is no argument against their being the work of the same man, for one finds a remarkable inequality in the standard of work produced by most of the smiths.

There is a most interesting pair of gates at Cote House, Oxon, bearing remains of an inscription and the date 1704 at the top of the overthrow (*Country Life*, Vol. xv, page 567). Writing of them, " Cygnus " says that the Hordes evidently clung to the old house, and he laments the fact that so many letters of the inscription are missing, letters which might provide evidence of value in elucidating the history of these exquisite gates (Fig. 80).

The fine series of chandelier hangers and the font cover crane, all from St. Michael's Church, Queenhythe, and now at the Victoria and Albert Museum, are exceedingly valuable examples of seventeenth century work. The hangers resemble each other closely, though graduated in elaboration. The same details, the twisting of the main square rods, the spiral tendrils

84 and 85.—CHANDELIER HANGERS, ST. MICHAEL'S CHURCH, QUEENHYTHE.
(*Victoria and Albert Museum.*)

running up the inside of the long scrolled leaves, and the large roses formed of circular plates with scalloped edges, riveted one over the other, occur in all three. In Fig. 84 we find an unusual feature in the conventional dragons' heads with forked tongues; in Fig. 85 a more elaborate centre rose and the addition of freely growing roses and tulips, which exhibit

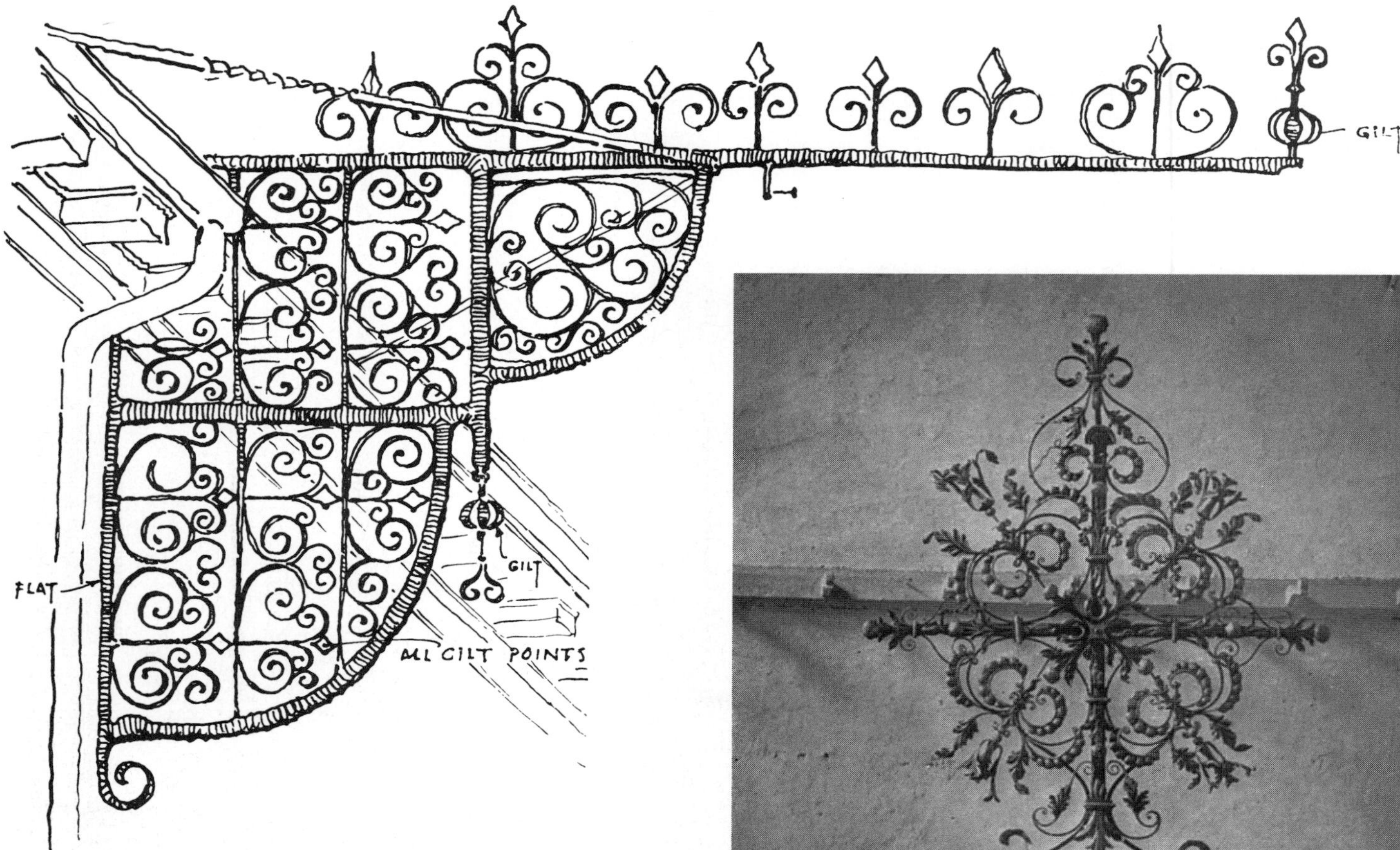

86.—SIGN BRACKET, OLIVER CROMWELL INN, ST. IVES.

87.—PORTION OF SWORD-REST, TREDEGAR CASTLE.

a distinct attempt towards naturalism strangely out of harmony with the four flat flowers cut out of iron sheet which grow from the base of the rose stems. A cluster of similar flat pomegranates will be seen in the cresting to the Wrexham choir rail just described. There is a repetition of them in Fig. 83, but with twisted stems, and there are also big, flat leaves with rudely scalloped edges, barely suggesting the acanthus they attempt to represent. These perfectly flat leaves and flowers are a characteristic feature of early seventeenth century work, and were probably originally painted in more or less realistic colours to give them the relief they otherwise lack. In some cases the veins of the leaves or petals were represented with chisel cuts. The smaller roses, their leaves and the tulip flowers in Fig. 83 are well modelled, and the whole commends itself as a fine piece of successful design. The workmanship is poor, the whole being riveted together in the clumsiest fashion. The font crane has little or no merit, and is only of interest in that it forms one of the series (Fig. 81). In not a single line does it suggest its use, and it owes so little to any principles of design or construction as to render criticism unnecessary. The workmanship is very inferior. In only one point does it better the hangers, *viz.*, that the bolt heads forming the centres to two of the roses are nicely worked. The actual date of the manufacture of these four pieces is not known. They are labelled as "late seventeenth century," but they might equally well have been made in 1650 or earlier.

The stand at Tredegar Castle has the appearance of a composite work, the upper part being the original, and possibly at one time a sword-rest or hanger. The detail closely resembles that of the ironwork from St. Michael's, Queenhythe.

While it is quite possible that such a large and important piece of ironwork as the north-west entrance gates to Tredegar Park Monument were entrusted to so

88.—STAIRCASE BALUSTRADE, CAROLINE PARK, MIDLOTHIAN.

eminent a smith as William Edney, there would appear to be no sufficient evidence to justify their being described as undoubtedly by W. Edney. In *English Ironwork of the Seventeenth and Eighteenth Centuries*, Mr. Starkie Gardner states that these gates are "undoubtedly by W. Edney."

The gates at Hampstead Marshall (Fig. 82) are interesting not only as a relic of the times before iron gates were commonly made and before the arrival of the decorative overthrow, but also because the wooden overthrow carries alternate spikes and a feature resembling ears of

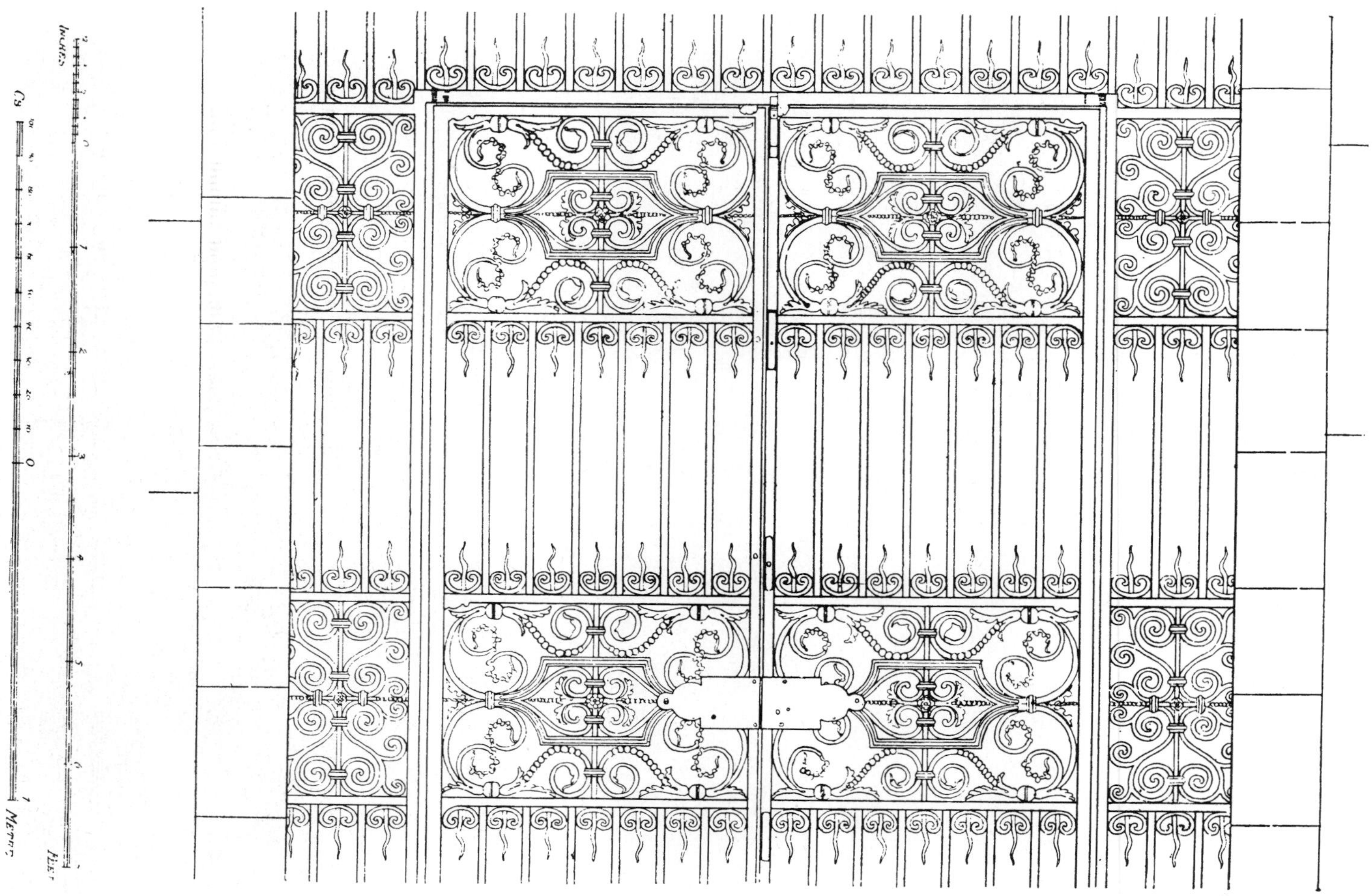

89.—DETAIL OF WROUGHT-IRON GATE, RIVER FRONT, TRINITY COLLEGE LIBRARY, CAMBRIDGE.

In the building accounts of Trinity College Library there is an item of £400 in favour of "Mr. Partridge, the London smith, for three iron gates in cloister and the iron railes in the staircase." This is the only record. The gates were erected in 1691, *and are of quite an unusual type of Renaissance ironwork.*

wheat, the spiral tendrils combined with the curling leaves of the latter being a feature which occurs in the Queenhythe ironwork.

In the gate to the river front of the Library, Trinity College, Cambridge, we have an attempt to produce a serious piece of architectural design in wrought ironwork which is singularly unsuccessful. It is poor both as a whole and in detail. The two horizontal bars are confusing, and it is not until one makes a close inspection that one finds that the upper one forms the top of the gate and that the apparent continuation of the vertical bars in reality forms the fixed grille to the space above the gate. Had the grille been a rich panel, and the upper part of the gate carried up in plain bars, the effect would have been better. The panels in the gates are the most satisfactory part of the design, but even these are only moderately successful, while those to the fixed side wings are distinctly bad, each having the defect of broken-backed scrolls, where the tendrils branch from the main scroll non-tangentially. The small C scrolls between the vertical bars, with their curling tongues, are similar to those at Traquair Castle and almost identical with those in two of the gateways at Ham House. a detail, happily, little used in the eighteenth century. When used as a pendant it is not objectionable, but used as it is here, both pendant and inverted, it has an uncomfortable appearance. The detail of the gates in no way helps matters. It might well be cast iron throughout, having all the hard, unsympathetic feeling of that medium when used without consideration of its limitations. The C scrolls already referred to are of too heavy iron and the diminution of them is too sudden. The scrolls to the side panels, though of greater importance, are, if anything, of lighter iron, but are again rigid and without life. The acanthus leaves to the main scrolls in the gate panels are dull in treatment, and the scalloped and bent fringe to the ends to the scrolls is, happily, not a form of enrichment which recommended itself to the smiths of the day as one to be repeated. The building accounts for the library include an item of £400 paid to "Mr. Partridge, the London smith, for three iron gates in cloister and the iron railes in the staircase." The gates were erected in 1691. They bear all the appearance of having been made from a design with which the smith, while anxious to give an exact rendering, was not in sympathy. It is careful work; but care without the feeling and knowledge necessary for vigorous handling must inevitably produce a dead thing.

90.—HOUR GLASS, ST. JOHN'S CHURCH ON THE WALL, BRISTOL.

Nothing could illustrate the reverse of this better than the balustrade to the staircase at Caroline Park, Midlothian (Fig. 88). The house was built by Viscount Tobart in 1685 and altered in 1696. The iron rail has the appearance of being part of the original building. Here we have wrought ironwork of surpassing merit and pulsating with life. It is a really fine treatment of the acanthus. There is something big and masterly in the handling of it, and the somewhat primitive forging only serves to accentuate its directness and vigour. As a design for a raking balustrade it is excellent. The great sweeping scrolls are cleverly given the appearance of interlacing by overlaying the vertical bars which form the panels, with the two open, four-petalled flowers and tendrils, and the whole effect is of a continuous rolling line, which leads the eye easily up the stair. Certain it is that the man who made it was a great artist, and it is a worthy example with which to close this chapter. While it is, perhaps, hardly representative of the seventeenth century prior to the arrival of William and Mary, yet, from the point of view of design, the freedom of the forging is typical of the smiths of this period. With later work we shall find greater accuracy and perfection of technique, but nowhere finer spirit.

APPENDIX I

"Anno vicesimo tertio Reginæ Elizabethæ. An Act touching Iron Mills near unto the city of London and the River Thames."

The above is the title of an Act which, after reciting the scarcity and "unreasonable" cost of timber, proceeds to lay down that from that time no one "shall convert or employ &c. to coal or other fewell for the making of iron, or of iron metal . . . any manner of wood or underwood now growing or which shall hereafter grow" within twenty-two miles of London or suburb of same or within twenty-two miles of the Thames from Dorchester downwards—nor within four miles of the "hills called the Downs, between Arundel and Pevensey," nor within four of Winchelsea and Rye, two of Pevensey and three of Hastings—"upon pain of forfeit for every load of wood so to be employed or converted into coal or other fewell for the making of iron . . . forty shillings of lawful money of England." It goes on to penalise new ironworks in the same area £100.

Another Act, passed in the twenty-seventh year of Elizabeth's reign, enacts that "no new iron w^{ks} shall be erected in Sussex Surrey or Kent—except where wr^{ks} already exist or where timber is grown on the same land purposely for the works—nor shall convert any sound timber 1 foot square at the stubb or any part—penalty £300 per iron w^{ks} 40/s per tree," excepting the "tops and offals" of trees outside the areas prescribed in the first Act, which may be used for making. iron; and further: "That the occupiers of all manner of iron works & which shall at any time hereafter carry any coals, mine, or iron between the 12th day of October and the 1st day of May yearly, shall likewise carry and lay for every six loads of coals, or mine, as well as also for every ton of iron which shall be carried by train or cart, by the space of one mile, through any highways under the hills, commonly called the North Downs of Surrey and Kent, to or from any iron works—one usual cart load of sinder, gravel, stone, sand, or chalk, meet for repairing the said high ways, under the direction of a Justice of the peace; or to pay for every such load which so ought to have been carried ij.s vjd to the hands of the said Justice of the peace—Statutes of the Realm, 27 Eliz. cap. 19." (*Some Account of the Worshipful Company of Ironmongers*, by John Nicholls, F.S.A., page 108).

APPENDIX II

From *Royal Society's Philosophical Transactions*, January and February, 1677–78. "An Account of the Iron Works in the Forest of Dean, communicated by Henry Powle, Esquire."

". . . The Ground is naturally inclined to Wood, especially Hasle and Oak; of which last sort it hath produced formally most stately Timber; though now, almost totally devoured by the increase of Iron Works. . . . The Iron Ore, which is the principal Manufacture here, and by which most of the Inhabitants subsist is found in great abundance in most parts of the Forest: differing both in colour, weight and goodness. The best, which they call their Brush ore, is of a Blewish colour; very ponderous, and full of little shining specks like grains of Silver. This affords the greatest quantity of Iron ; but being melted alone produceth a Metal very short and brittle, and therefore not so fit for common use.

"To remedy this inconveniency, they make use of another Sort of Material, which they call their Cynder, and is nothing else but the Refuse of the Ore after the Metal hath been Extracted ; which being mingled with the other in due quantity, gives it that excellent temper of Toughness, for which this Iron is preferred before any that is brought from Foreign parts.

"But to understand this rightly, it is to be noted, That in former times, when their works were few, and their Vent small, they made use of no other Bellows, but such as were moved by the strength of men : by reason whereof their Fires were much less intense, than the Furnaces they now employ. So that having in them melted down only the principal part of the Ore ; they rejected the rest as useless, and not worth their charge. This they call their Cynder, which is now found in an inexhaustible quantity through all parts of the Country, where any former Works have stood. After they have provided their Ore, their first work is to Calcine it : which is done in Kilns, much after the fashion of our ordinary Lime-Kilns. These they fill up to the top with Coal and Ore, *stratum super stratum*, until it be full ; and so putting Fire to the bottom, they let it burn till the Coal be wasted, and then renew the kilns with fresh Ore and Coal, in the same manner as before. This is done without Fushion of the Metal, and serves to consume the more drossy parts of the Ore, and to make it friable ; supplying the Beating and Washing, which are used to other Metals. From hence they carry it to their Furnaces which are built of Brick and Stone, about 24 foot square on the outside, and near 30 foot in height. Within, not above 8 or 10 foot over, where it is widest, which is about the middle ; the top and bottom having a narrower compass, much like the shape of an Egg, as in the Figure. *See Fig.* 4. A. *the Tunnel*, C *the Furnace*, B *the Mouth of the Furnace*.

"Behind the Furnace are placed two huge pair of Bellows, whose Noses meet at a little hole near the bottom. These are compressed together by certain Buttons, placed on the Axis of a very large wheel, which is turn'd about by water, in the manner of an Overshot Mill. As soon as these Buttons are slid off, the Bellows are raised again by the counterpoise of weights ; whereby they are made to play alternately, the one giving its blast all the time the other is rising. At first, they fill these Furnaces with Ore and Cynder intermixed with Fuel, which in these Works is always of Charcoal ; laying them hollow at the bottom, that they may more easily take fire. But after they are once kindled, the Materials run together into a hard cake or lump, which is sustained by the fashion of the Furnace, and through this the Metal, as it melts, trickles down into the Receivers, which are placed at the bottom, where there is a passage open, by which they take away the Scum and Dross, and let out the Metal as they see Occasion. Before the Mouth of the Furnace, lies a great Bed of Sand, wherein they make Furrows of the fashion into which they desire to cast their Iron. Into these, when their Receivers are full, they let in their Metal ; which is made so very fluid by the violence of the Fire, that it not only runs to a considerable distance ; but stands afterwards boiling for a good while. After these Furnaces are once at work, they keep them constantly employed for many months together, never suffering the Fire to slacken night nor day ; but still supplying the waste of the Fuel and other Materials with fresh, poured in at the top. Several attempts have been made to bring in the use of Sea coal in these Works, instead of Charcoal ; the former being to be had at an easie rate, the latter, not without great expense, but hitherto they have proved ineffectual. The workmen finding by experience, that a Sea-coal Fire, how vehement soever, will not penetrate the most fixed parts of the Ore, and so leaveth much of the Metal unmelted. From these Furnaces, they bring their Sows and Pigs of Iron (as they call them) to their Forges. These are of two sorts, though standing together under the same Roof : one they call their Finery, the other the Chafery. Both of them are open Hearths, on which they place great heaps of sea-Coal, and behind them Bellows, like to those of the Furnaces, but nothing near so large. Into the Finery, they first put their Pigs of Iron, placing three or four of them, together behind the fire, with a little of one end thrust into it. Where softening by degrees they stir and work them with long Bars of Iron, till the Metal runs together into a round Mass or Lump, which they call a Half Bloom. This they take out, and giving it a few strokes with their Sledges, they carry it to a great weighty Hammer, raised likewise by the motion of a Water-wheel : where applying it dexterously to the blows, they perfectly beat it out into a thick short square. This they put into the Finery again, and heating it red hot, they work it out under the same Hammer, till it comes into the shape of a Bar in the middle with two square Knobs in the ends. Last of all they give it other Heatings in the Chafery and more workings under the Hammer, till they have brought their Iron into Bars of several shapes and sizes ; in which fashion they expose them to Sale. All their Principal Iron undergoes all the fore mentioned preparations : yet for several purposes, as for the Backs of Chimneys, Hearths of Ovens, and the like, they have a sort of Cast Iron ; which they take out of the Receivers of the Furnace so soon as it is melted, in great Ladles, and pour it into Moulds of fine Sand : in like manner as they cast Brass and other softer Metals : but this sort of Iron is so very brittle, that being heated, with one blow of a Hammer it breaks all to pieces. Though this fault be most found in this sort of Iron ; yet if in the working of their Best sort they omit any one Process it will be sure to want some part of its Toughness, which they esteem its perfection."

APPENDIX III

"England's Improvements by Sea and Land to Out-do the Dutch without Fighting to Pay Debts without Moneys—by Andrew Yarranton, Gent.—London—1677."

Pages 56–63 : " And First, I will begin in *Monmouthshire*, and go through the Forest of Deane, and there take notice what infinite quantities of Raw Iron is there made, with Bar Iron and Wire ; and consider the infinite number of Men, Horses, and Carriages which are to supply these Works, and also digging of Iron Stone, providing of cinders, carrying to the Works, making it into Sows and Bars, . . .

" Moreover, there is yet a most great benefit to the Kingdom in general by the Sow Iron made of the Iron Stone and Roman Cinders in the Forest of Dean ; for that Metal is of a most gentle, pliable, soft nature, easily and quickly to be wrought into Manufacture, over what any other Iron is, and it is the best in the known World : and the greatest part of this Sow Iron is sent up Severne to the *Forges*, into *Worcester-shire*, *Shropshire*, *Stafford-shire*, *Warwick-shire* and *Cheshire*, and there it's made into Bar Iron : And because of its kind and gentle nature to work, it is now at *Sturbridge*, *Dudley*, *Wolverhampton*, *Sedgley*, *Walsall*, and *Burmingham*, and thereabouts wrought and manufactured into all small Commodities, and diffused all *England* over, and thereby a great Trade made of it ; and when manufactured, sent into most parts of the World—And I can very easily make it appear, that in the Forest of *Deane*, and thereabouts, and about the Materials that come from thence, there are employed, and have their subsistance therefrom, no less than sixty thousand persons. And certainly if this be true, then it is certain it is better these Iron-works were up and in being, than that there were none. . . . And now in *Worcester-shire*, *Shropshire*, *Stafford-shire*, *Warwick-shire* and *Derby-shire* there are great and numerous quantities of Iron-works, and there much Iron is made of Metal or Iron Stone, of another nature quite different from that of the Forest of *Deane*. This Iron is short soft Iron commonly called Cold-shore Iron, of which all the Nails are made, and infinite other Commodities : In which work are employed many more persons, if not double to what are employed in the Forest of *Deane*. . . .

" The next Objection is, That is was better when there was no Iron made in *England ;* But when that was, neither I nor the Objector knows—For in the Forest of *Deane* and thereabouts the Iron is made at this day of Cinders, being the rough and offal thrown by in the *Romans* times ; they having only foot blasts to melt the Iron Stone, but now by the force of a Great Wheel that drives a pair of Bellows twenty foot long, all that Iron is extracted out of the Cinders which could not be forced from it by the *Roman* Foot-blast. And in the Forest of *Deane* and thereabouts, and as high as Worcester, there are great and infinite quantities of these Cinders ; some in vast Mounts above ground, some under ground, which will supply the Iron-Works. Some hundreds of years, and these cinders are they which make the prime and best Iron, and with much less Charcoal than doth the Iron Stone. . . .

" Now I have shewed you the two Manufactures of Linen and Iron with the product thereof, and all the materials are with us growing ; and these two Manufactures will if by Law countenanced set all the poor in *England* at work, and much inrich the Country, and thereby fetch people into the Kingdom, whereas now they depart ; and thereby deprive the *Dutch* of these two great Manufactures of Iron and Linen : I mean Iron wrought in all Commodities, so vastly brought down the *Rhine* into *Holland* from *Liege*, *Gluke*, *Soley* and *Cologne*, and by them diffused and sent all the World over. . . .

" And as to the Incouragement of the Iron, and Iron Manufactures, there should be three pound a Tun Custom, laid on all foreign Bar Iron imported, and six pounds the Tun on all the Manufactured Iron imported into England ; and by these two ways, namely by a Tax being laid upon the imported Bar Iron, Iron Wares, and Thread, Tape, Twine, and Linen Cloth of all sorts, all the Trade of these things will be here, and all the Poor set at work, the Dutch robbed of one of their greatest Flowers and to the King and people in general at least six Millions a year advantage."

CHAPTER V

JEAN TIJOU

IN 1684 the total manufacture of iron in England only slightly exceeded ten thousand tons a year. Macaulay, writing upon the Acts of the reign of Queen Elizabeth already referred to, says :

> At the close of the reign of Charles II a great part of the iron which was used in this Country was imported from abroad, and the whole quantity made here annually seems to have exceeded ten thousand tons.

By 1740, however, a little over half a century, the output had increased to the astounding figure of one hundred and eighty thousand tons ; and it is during this exact period that decorative ironwork flourished to an extent unequalled before or since. From being a medium practically

91.—PANEL FROM FOUNTAIN SCREEN, HAMPTON COURT PALACE.

92.—DETAIL OF TOP OF FOUNTAIN SCREEN.

93.—PANEL FROM FOUNTAIN SCREEN, HAMPTON COURT PALACE.

94.—IRELAND.

95.—SCOTLAND.

unconsidered by the architects and their patrons, it suddenly, with the arrival of William and Mary, leapt to the forefront and became one of the characteristic features of the architecture of the day.

The last quarter of the seventeenth century was the period of the greatest activity in the building world that has, probably, ever been experienced in England.

96.—ENGLAND.

97.—WALES.

FOUR PANELS FROM THE FOUNTAIN SCREEN, HAMPTON COURT PALACE.

From the buildings of the Early Renaissance remaining to us all over the country, and from the writings of the times, we know how universal was the interest then taken by every cultured person in architecture. The release from the severity and restrictions enforced by Puritanism upon all display of wealth was heralded by an anxiety on every hand, by all possessed of means, to vie with one another in providing for themselves habitations of the most magnificent description. This inclination received the strongest impetus in the enforced rebuilding of London after the Great Fire of 1666, which afforded an opportunity to the genius of Sir Christopher Wren such as has been accorded to no other architect before or since. We are to be congratulated as a nation that we had at hand such a brain as his to carry on the movement of the Renaissance.

The use of wrought ironwork as a factor in decorative architectural work came late in the French Renaissance and, as has already been stated, we followed in our neighbours' footsteps in this respect.

Wren, travelling in 1665, wrote a delightful letter from Paris, addressed to " a particular friend," from which we may assume that the wonderful ironwork being made there at that time, under Marot and others, was occupying some of his attention, for he says :

> I have purchas'd a great deal of *Taille-douce* that I might give our Countrymen examples of Ornaments and Grotesks, in which the Italians themselves confess the French to excel. I hope I shall give you a very good account of all the best Artists of France ; my business now is to pry into Trades and Arts. I put myself into

98.—GATES, EAST FRONT, HAMPTON COURT PALACE.

99.—RAILINGS TO RIVER, HAMPTON COURT PALACE.

all shapes to humour them ; 'tis a Comedy to me, and tho' sometimes expenceful, I am loth yet to leave it. —*Parentalia*.

It was not, however, until many years later that he commenced to use ironwork to any extent, an omission which he fully repaired when once he began.

As we have seen, there were many indications not only that the smiths were ready and only waiting for a lead to be given them, but that considerable interest was still maintained throughout the country in the trade. So far, however, it had been allowed to simmer only, and there were no defined lines upon which the smiths could work or their patrons give their orders. That the feeling for it was there was proved later by the immediate response made by the English smiths to the fashions introduced from Holland by the new King.

The effect upon the industry of the arrival of William and Mary cannot be over-estimated, and it did no less than give birth to a most interesting and brilliant phase in the history of wrought iron. The beauty of Hampton Court, with its great waterway boundary and formal canal and fountains, appealed instantly to the Hollander and his Queen, and one can well imagine their becoming more reconciled to their enforced life in England when they had decided to make this their chief residence.

An immediate start was made upon the new wing by Sir Christopher Wren, who, with the accession of William and Mary, had retained his appointment of H.M. Surveyor-General of Works, made by Charles II. A temporary lodging, called the Water Gallery, was first erected for the use of the Queen until such time as the main buildings were completed. Our interest lies for the moment, however, in the alterations in the garden, the most important feature of which

100.—CENTRE GATE, EAST FRONT, HAMPTON COURT PALACE.

101.—SIDE GATE, EAST FRONT, HAMPTON COURT PALACE.

was to be a great wrought-iron screen to the Fountain Court, an entirely new departure in England, and one which was to have far-reaching effects.

No doubt, realising that he would be unable to obtain what he required of English smiths, William brought with him, or was immediately followed by, a smith named Jean Tijou, a Frenchman by birth and a man of such talent and energy that, after twenty-one years' work in

102.—CENTRE GATES, SOUTH FRONT, HAMPTON COURT PALACE.

103.—SIDE GATES, SOUTH FRONT, HAMPTON COURT PALACE.

104.—DOOR PANEL, NORTH SIDE, SOUTH CHOIR AISLE, ST. PAUL'S CATHEDRAL.

105.—PANEL FROM CHORISTERS' DESK, CHAPEL OF SS. MICHAEL AND GEORGE, ST. PAUL'S CATHEDRAL.

England, he was acknowledged father of the English school of seventeenth and eighteenth century smithing.

In view of his importance in the history of ironwork, it is particularly fortunate that recent years have disclosed a quantity of documentary evidence concerning him—more, in fact, than exists of any other known smith of the period.

The discovery some years ago of a book, published in 1693, entitled *A New Booke of Drawings Invented and Desined by John Tijou*, has led to his being placed upon a pinnacle of greater eminence than he deserves, or, perhaps, it would be fairer to say, that it has conduced to his being looked upon too much as the one fount of inspiration from which our English smiths drew. Nevertheless, no man has left his mark more definitely stamped upon the history of his trade than Tijou. His method of working, his fondness for certain *motifs*, his extravagant use of modelled leafwork and his elaborate *repoussé* panels and masks are so characteristic as to render the recognition of his handiwork a simpler matter than is the case with work by other smiths of his time. The marvellous dexterity he possessed led him to over-elaboration, a temptation he could not resist. An examination of his work shows that he refused to allow the material in which he worked to guide or control the riot of his imagination. His technical skill carried him through the difficulties he designed for himself, and he depended upon this for his success, which he obtained rather in spite of the material than by the aid of it. In some examples of his work, notably the great screen at Hampton Court originally made for the Fountain Garden, one cannot help feeling that he was, first and foremost, a *repoussé* worker and a smith incidentally. His faults and merits are alike startlingly apparent in this particular piece of work, one of his most important, and one in which he was evidently given full freedom. There are twelve panels similar to those illustrated, each about 10ft. 6ins. high and just over 13ft. wide, the centre of each being filled with some emblem of Royalty. The panels being spaced with wide intervals of palisade and plain dog-bars, it is not unfair to criticise them as individual compositions, and, as such, they are unpleasing. They call for some connecting overhead frame, and the general shape is squat and undignified. The size of the acanthus leaves and festoon of husks is overpowering and out of scale with the lighter enrichments ; the scantling, too, of the iron bar used in the smaller scrollwork is rendered flimsy by the heavy vertical lines of the enclosing piers ; nor, in this instance, is the introduction of bay or laurel leaves happy. This work may well exemplify the persistence or recurrence of the *motifs* of previous generations, and with these Tijou may have been preoccupied while in sole charge and, as yet, without the restraining and inspiring influence of Wren. There is a seeming desire to crowd the whole surface with enrichment without regard to its effect as a whole, and one would turn away were it not for the fascination of the well-nigh superhuman dexterity with which he made these pieces of iron subservient to his will. The screen is, indeed, a stupendous effort, and one recognises with astonishment the full-blooded, voluptuous animal in the man who

106.—THE GOLDEN GATES : SANCTUARY SCREEN (NORTH), ST. PAUL'S CATHEDRAL.

conceived it. Happily, it may be seen erected once more, after many vicissitudes, at Hampton Court, at the end of the Privy Garden.

This screen, with the gates, consisting of "twelve pannells," also "pillars of ornaments," pilasters, etc., including iron and workmanship, cost £2,160 2s. 0¼d., according to the Hampton Court accounts, 1689–96.

Turning to the gates in the east front, one sees at once the presence of the controlling mind of the architect, where the best in the smith is turned to good account in the rendering of a fine

107.—GOLDEN GATES, SANCTUARY SCREEN (SOUTH), ST. PAUL'S CATHEDRAL.

design. No loose display here, but the quiet, dignified treatment of a master. And so it is with all important work which he carried out under Sir Christopher Wren. The examples of his work to be found in St. Paul's Cathedral, though so close at hand, are little known to Londoners. Like the gates just mentioned, a glance is sufficient to show their immense superiority in the quality of design over that of the Fountain screen.

While it has been admitted that Wren exerted a great influence over Tijou, the actual designing of the ironwork, both in the Palace at Hampton Court and in St. Paul's, has been generally attributed to the smith. It is impossible, however, to reconcile the masterly architectural treatment of the important work in these two buildings with Tijou's somewhat crude efforts when unguided. The power and ability to design any portion of a building require equal knowledge and experience, and it is unreasonable to imagine that Wren would be content to place in the hands of a smith such important factors in the scheme of his buildings as are illustrated

108 and 109.—DETAILS OF REPOUSSÉ PANELS FROM SANCTUARY SCREEN (NORTH), ST. PAUL'S CATHEDRAL.

here. It is not suggested, however, that full-size detail drawings, such as are necessary now, were made by Wren. The following extract from the original accounts, indeed, proves, if it is necessary, that this was not the case :

> Aug. 1796 To Charles Hopson Joyner ffor time spent for gluing of Boards for Mr Tijoue to draw ye Iron Screen &c upon.

But that careful drawings of every detail of importance were supplied by Wren is certain.

110.—GATES AND SCREEN TO NORTH CHOIR AISLE, ST. PAUL'S CATHEDRAL.

111.—CANDELABRA GATES (NORTH SIDE), ST. PAUL'S CATHEDRAL.

NOTE.—*The north gates* (*Fig.* 111) *and screen without the candelabra are clearly shown on an original scale drawing in Wren's album. It is a section through the east end, looking south, and is drawn in brown or faded ink and pencil.*

The north and south sanctuary screens are made up from the original organ or choir screen, removed about 1860, when it was, unfortunately, deemed necessary to alter the arrangement of the choir by moving the stalls one bay farther west. The alteration left the bay nearest the east end open, and in 1890 the present screens were erected. The organ originally stood upon eight marble columns, four on the nave side and four in the choir. Between the two centre ones on the nave side were the magnificent double gates now in the centre of the north screen, and

112.—ORIGINAL ALTAR RAIL, ST. PAUL'S CATHEDRAL.

on either side of them, as fixed grilles, were the two leaves of what now forms the centre portion of the south screen. The fixed grille on the left of the illustration, and a duplicate of it in the south screen, formed the sides of the passage-way under the organ to the choir. The whole of the brass and iron work not mentioned in the foregoing is modern, and was added in 1890 at the time of re-erection. The space between the top of the gates and the underside of the organ was originally filled with a frieze of iron panels, which is now to be seen, together with four of the marble columns, utilised as an internal porch at the north entrance of the cathedral. An examination of the original building accounts for August, 1696, reveals the following :

To John Tijoue Smith ffor ye Iron Screen under ye Organ case in ye Choire containing 221 foot superficiall at 40sh. p. foot by Contract 442 00 00

—only one instance of many showing the very large remuneration commanded by such works of art at that time, as compared with the present day. Allowing for the variation in the purchasing power of money then and now, the cost represents a sum of not less than £3,000 of our money.

113.—GATE AT FIRST LANDING OF GEOMETRICAL STAIR, ST. PAUL'S CATHEDRAL.

114.—TERMINAL TO GUARD RAIL, FIRST LANDING OF GEOMETRICAL STAIR, ST. PAUL'S CATHEDRAL.

In April, 1699, an entry in the accounts reads :

To John Tijou Smith ffor two Desks for ye Choristers 9 foot long each containing 26 pannills 16 inches square by agreement £265 - 00 - 00

These panels were stored, until recently, in the crypt, but are now admirably used in the new seating in the Chapel of St. Michael and St. George. There are twelve repetitions of the panel illustrated, and ten of floral and strapwork design. They are of exceedingly thin metal worked almost entirely from the front, while the iron was cold, probably beaten up roughly from the back first and the background cut away when the panel was complete. Upon either side, across the north and south aisles dividing the nave from the presbytery, are two screens which aligned with the organ screen. Their position between the massive stonework required a heavier treatment than that adopted for the former, and in them we have ironwork used with consummate skill. The weight and scale are perfect, and the arrangement of the triple pyramid overthrow is most ingenious. The workmanship throughout is most masterly. For these two screens, erected in June, 1705, Tijou received £540.

115.—CHORISTERS' DESK, CHAPEL OF ST. MICHAEL AND ST. GEORGE, ST. PAUL'S CATHEDRAL.

The present choir screen is the original communicants' rail, removed from the east end in 1860 and relegated to the crypt until many years later, when it was brought to light once more and took the place of some very inferior modern brass railings. Made in 1707, it was fixed in June of that year at a cost of £260. The rail, for its whole length, is a repetition of the panels illustrated, and is not of the same standard of design as the work already referred to, but this is far from condemning it as unworthy.

116.—PANEL TO STAIRCASE LANDING, 35 LINCOLN'S INN FIELDS.
Whilst there is no evidence that this is the work of Tijou, it bears all the marks of his handiwork.

As fine architectural ironwork, it would be difficult to name anything to surpass the guard-rail at the first landing of the geometrical stair. It takes its place so naturally on the stone parapet that the eye travels over it without being arrested by the change in material. To suggest that

117.—GATES, CLARENDON PRESS, OXFORD.

the design for this stone and iron work was not the product of one brain is not justifiable, and there remains sufficient merit in having executed the latter for one to be conscious of no unfairness in ascribing only the workmanship to Tijou.

Other examples might be given, some authentic, such as the ironwork at Burleigh House, Stamford; and some merely ascribed to Tijou, such as that at Drayton House, Northampton. In the foregoing descriptions and illustrations, however, are shown the best and the most typical manifestations of his genius.

118.—BALUSTRADE TO STAIRCASE, 35 LINCOLN'S INN FIELDS.

APPENDIX

EXTRACTS FROM BUILDING ACCOUNTS OF ST. PAUL'S CATHEDRAL, SHOWING THE AMOUNTS PAID TO TIJOU AND OTHERS FOR VARIOUS IRONWORK.

"Charges of work done for and towards the rebuilding of the Cathedral Church of St. Paul's London" during October 1st, 1689, to the last of September, 1690.

Ann Salter—for cross garnetts, nails, bolts &c.
Samuele Coalburne smith—for mending tools, supplying wedges &c, cramps & odd smith's work generally attending other trades.
Thomas Hodgkins, smith— do do.
Nicholas Broock, smith— do do.

Under heading of "Provisions," October 1st, 1690, to September 30th, 1691.

Mar. 19, 1691 — Mounsr. Tijoue for two round Iron windows for the Great West Door att £6 each by contract 12.00.00
Wittness, Jno. Widows. *Rec'd J. Tijou.*

Aug., 1691 — To Mounsr. Tijou ffor the Ironwork of the ffirst window to the South East of the Quire; according to a contract Dated June 30th 1691 (vizt.) ffor 18c:0qr:7lb at 6d p lb 50.11.06
ffor 45 foot runing of the Grotesk barrs at 6sh p foot 13.10.c0
ffor the workmanship of the Scrowle in the Key 03.00.00

Sept. 27th '95. 67.01.c6
Wittness, J. Widows. *Rec. J. Tijou.*

From account October 1st, 1691, to September 30th, 1692.

Nov., 1691 — To Monsr. Tijoue ffor the Iron Work of two windows for ye choirs vizt.
ffor 34c 1qr 20lb at 6d p lb .. 96.08.00
ffor 45 foot runing of the Grotesk barrs at 6s per foot 13.10.00
ffor 45 foot runing of Grotesk barrs being different from ye rest at 4s p foot runing 09.00.00
ffor workmanship of ye two scrowles in ye Keys 06.00.00

Sept. 27th '95 124.18.00
Wittnesse, J. Widdows. *Recdd. p J. Tijou.*

Jan., 1691–2 — To Monsr. Tijoue ffor the Ironwork of six windows vizt.—
ffor 100c 2qr 2lb at 6d p lb .. 281.09.00
ffor 270 foot runing of the Grotesk barrs at 4s pr. foot 054.00.00
ffor workmanship of the Six Scrowles in the Keys 018.00.00

Sept. 27th '95 353.00.00
Wittnesse, J. Widows. *Recdd. p J. Tijou.*

May, 1692 — To Monsr. Tijoue ffor the Iron work of six windowes vizt.—
ffor 111c 1qr 21lb att 6d p lb .. 312.00.06
ffor 270 foot runing of the Grotesk barrs at 4s each 054.00.00
ffor workmanship of the six scrowles in the Keys 018.00.00

Sept. 27th '95 384.00.06
Wittnesse, J. Widows. *Recdd. p J. Tijou.*

And in the same month, under "Carriages":
Paid to John Seyford ffor litherage, wharfage, cranage —
ffor carriage of 4 iron windows to the Church 00.06.00

October 1st, 1692, to September 30th, 1693.

Nov., 1692 — To Monsr. Tijoue ffor the Ironwork of ffour windows wt. 72c 1qr 11lb at 6d p lb 202.11.06
ffor 180 foot runing of ye Grotesk barrs at 4sh p foot 036.00.00
ffor workmanship of ye ffour scrowles in ye Keys 012.00.00
Sept. 27th '95
Wittnesse, J. Widows. *Recdd. p J. Tijou*

And the same month for carriage as before:
ffor cartage of 4 Iron windows to the Church 00.08.00
To John Seyford.

January, 1693, William Webster, smith, and Richard Howes, smith, appear for general ironwork as Coleburn.

May, 1693 — To Mr. John Tijoue, Smith, ffor the Ironwork of three upper windows at

the East end, wt. 34c 00qr 10lb at 6d p lb 95.09.00
ffor 24 Roses at — each

This entry is cancelled; the last item is written in a very inferior handwriting.

Under "Carriages" in the same month, however, Seyford is paid—

ffor cartage of three Iron windows to ye Church 00.05.00

October 1st, 1693, to September 30th, 1694.

Nov., 1693 — To Monsr. Tijoue ffor Ironwork for ye 3 upper windows, at ye East end of ye Choire, wt. 39c 3qr 4lb at 6d p lb 111.08.00
ffor 24 Roses at 5s each 06.00.00
ffor 90 foot run of ye Grotesk Barrs at 4s p foot 18.00.00

Sept. 27th, 1693. 135.08.00

Wittnesse, J. Widows *Recdd. p J. Tijou*

March, 1694 — To John Tijoue ffor the Ironwork of six upper windows in the choire, wt. 76c 1qr 12lb at 6d 213.16.00
ffor 192 foot runing of the Grotesk Barrs at 4s p foot 38.08.00

Sept. 27th, '95. 252.04.00

Wittnesse, J. Widows. *Recdd. p J. Tijou*

A deduction is made from Coalburne's account as follows:

May, 1694 — Deduct ffor Old Iron delivered, wt. 14c 0qr 21lb at 12s p c

August, again more is deducted at 12s. from Richard Hows' account.

Sept. — To Richard Hows, Smith, ffor Ironwork for ffour windows over the South side Isle of ye Choire, wt. 8c 2qrs 5lb at 5d* p lb 19.18.09
ffor 4 Casements and fframes, wt. 1c 3qrs 9lb at 8½d† 07.05.02½
To Thomas Coalburne, Smith, ffor new Barrs for one of ye windows over ye North side Isle of the Choire, wt. 2c 2qr 4lb at 5d‡ p lb .. 05.18.04
ffor new casements and fframe, wt. 0c 2qr 3lb at 8½d‡ p lb 02.01.09½

*Has originally been put in at 6d. and altered to 5d.
†Has originally been put in at 9d. and altered to 8½d.
‡Have also been altered as above. Entries at this price continue to appear after this date.

October 1st, 1694, to September 30th, 1695.

October — To John Tijoue ffor Ironwork of the Rayles of Two Staire cases in Mr. Thompson & Mr. Ffulke's work .. 40.00.00
ffor two little windows in ye said staire cases 20.00.00

Sept. 27th, '95 60.00.00

Wittnesse, J. Widdows. *Recdd. p J. Tijou.*

To Samuell Ffulkes ffor 5 days work of a mason in cutting of holes for ye Ironwork of ye little stairs case in his work at 2sh 6d p day 00.12.06
ffor 6 days work of a mason in taking downe the Arch and cutting way for a window in the head of the Neech in ye said little staire-case at 2sh 6d p day 00.15.00

NOTE.—Small cramps were charged for at 3¾d.

October 1st, 1695, to September 30th, 1696.

March, 1696 — To John Tijoue, Smith, ffor work done in the side ffronts of the Joyners work in ye choire (Grotesk-work), ffor 10 Pannills each 3 foot by two foot 11 inches, containing in all 58 foot 3 inches superficial at 40s p foot 116.10.00
ffor 6 Pannills, each 2 foot 2 inches by 1 foot 11 inches and ½, containing in all 29 foot 3ins at 40s p foot superficiall 58.10.00
ffor 4 Pannills each 2 foot 10 inches and ½ by 2 ft. 9 inches, containing in all 31 foot 7 inches at 40s p foot superficiall 63.03.04
ffor 16 Pannills, 2 foot 4 inches and ½ by 1 foot 6 inches and ½, containing in all 58 foot at 40s per foot superficiall 116.00.00

354.03.04

Recdd. p. J. Tijou.

No date.

May, 1696 — To John Tijoue Smith, Smith, ffor adding ffour yards of iron railing on the top of the little staires in Mr. Thompson & Mr. Ffulke's work at ye West end of the Church 04.00.00

Reced. p. J. Tijou.

No date.

Task Work.

August — To John Tijoue, Smith, ffor ye Iron screen under ye Organ case in ye Choire, 221 foot superficiall at 40sh. p foot by contract 442.00.00

Reced. p. J. Tijou.

No date.

To Charles Hopson, Joyner, ffor time spent and staffe used in making . . . [here come various " modells "] and for gluing of boards for Mr. Tijoue to draw ye Iron Screen &c upon and gluing of Boards for Mr. Gibbons to draw on . . .

October 1st, 1696, to September 30th, 1697.

July, 1697	To Thomas Robinson, Smith, ffor 2 paire of hinges for the Communion Table Raile door, and 32 screws, wt. 64 lb at 10d	02.13.04
	ffor 8 square pillors of iron 3 foot long with nutts and screws for ye same Raile, wt. 2 qrs 23 lb at 6d p	01.19.06
	ffor 36 Holdfasts for ye morning prayer Chapell	00.09.00
	July 28th, '99.	05.01.10

Wittness, Jno. Widdows *Reced. p. Thomas Robinson.*

October 1st, 1697, to September 30th, 1698.

Dec., 1697	To Thomas Robinson, smith, ffor 3 Engines for the pulpit	10.00.00
	ffor a paire of Hinges with screws, revits and nailes for the door of the pulpit	00.10.00
	ffor 10 squares and 18 wood screws	00.09.00
	ffor a new Lock and Screws and Shutting Plate	00.18.00
		11.17.00
October	To Thomas Robinson ffor 32 small cramps for his pillors in the morning chappell at 9d each	01.04.00
	ffor 36 Holdfasts for ye morning prayr. Chappell ( ) fashon ..	00.12.00
	ffor a mask and cup for my Lord Mayor's Sword and gilding them..	01.12.06
	And various other items (22 in all) Total £17.	
	To Mary Sherlock, widdow, ffor Iron monges. ware vizt. . . .	
	ffor 167 Brass spikes for ye Communion Raile at 10d each	06.19.02
	To John Tijou, Smith, a years interest of 500£ due 29th Sept. '97 as p. Receipt in ye Acquittance Book	30.00.00
Jan., 1698	To Thomas Robinson ffor a paire of Hinges for ye Hatches of the morning prayr. Chappell	01.04.00
	ffor mending one of the Locks of the Iron gates under the Organ ..	00.01.00
	To the said Thomas Robinson, Smith, for Iron work for ye windows in ye 2 staire cases at ye North and South East ends of the Choire and for ye windows in ye rooms over the north and south east vestreys, wt. 8c 1qr 13lb. at 7d	27.06.07
	ffor 10 Rows of spikes and 4 Scrowles and plates and nailes for the Gallaries in the Choire	04.10.00
	Altogether 39 items totalling ..	23.06.11
		52.12.06
June, 1698	To Thomas Robinson, Smith, ffor two large iron railes for ye seats in ye organ Loft	
	ffor 12 scrowles with stays for ye same and screws	24.00.00
	Altogether 16 items amounting to	£32.09.00
July	To Thomas Robinson, Smith, ffor an Iron Raile for ye Morning Prayer Chappell containing 43 foot in length and 121 Hollow Spikes and Balls and 136 Plaine spikes and scrowles and 4 doors with Hinges and Bolts and Lock, wt. 22c 1qr 27lb at 10s p lb ..	104.19.02
	ffor . . . . Lock with 4 Keys and Brass plates and screws for ye wooden dores, and ye Hinges of ye ffour Iron dores with Bolts and fixing ye work to ye marbles	005.00.00
	July 28th, '99.	

Wittness, Jno. Widdow *Recd. p. Thomas Robinson.*

NOTE.—There are about 39ft. of rail and 107 spikes.

July, 1698	To John Tijoue, Smith, ffor two Great Gates on ye north and south side at ye east end of ye Choire, containing 354 foot in both superficiall at 40s p. foot..	708.00.00
	ffor two Little round windows looking into the staire Cases on ye north and south sides at ye east end of the Choire at £5 each	010.00.00
	ffor ye great Gates on ye outside of ye Church Leading to ye East side of ye South portico and a wicket in ye middle of it fframed with strong iron and ornaments with points ..	160.00.00
	Ffor iron work for 6 windows for ye north and south crosses of ye Dome, wt. 98c 3qr at 6d p lb	276.10.00
July, 1698	ffor 200 foot of Ornaments in ye said windows at 4s p. foot runing ..	40.00.00
	ffor the two little Gates Joyning to ye screen, containing in both 210 foot at 40ch p. foot	430.00.00
	Aug. 29th, '99.	1614.10.00

Wittnesse, Jno. Widdows. *Received p. J. Tijou.*

In the same account appears an entry paid to Seyford:

	ffor carriage of 2 and upwards of ironwork for ye Morning Prayr. Chappell, from Ffetter Lane to ye Church	00.08.00

October 1st, 1698, to September 30th, 1699.

Oct.	To Thomas Robinson, Smith, are 16 items, amounting to £17.05.00.	
	To the said Countesse Dowager of Northampton asignee of Mr. Seyford, Mr. Tijou and Mr. Beauchampe, principall money at p. ye severall Indentures cancelled appeare ..	1550.00.00
Jan.	A/c 32 items amounting to 15.12.05 to Robinson, and another of 8 items for £04.15.01.	
April	To John Tijou, smith, ffor a paire of great Gates at ye west side of the south portico with a wicket framed of strong iron with ornaments and points on ye top	160.00.00
	ffor two Desks for ye Choristers 9 foot long each, containing 26 panills 16 inches square, wt. in both 6c 00qr 6lb and for 4 Brackets for ye same, containing about 24 foot sup. f., wt. 2c 2qr 12lb by agreement	265.00.00
	August 21st, 1700.	425.00.00

Wittnesse, Jno. Widdows. Received p. J. Tijou.

In an account to Robinson there is an item:

	ffor 32 cast windows for ye Dome at 7s each	11.04.00

In Seyford's account appears:

	ffor carriage of 2 iron Gates from Piccadilly to ye Church	00.10.00

Account to Thomas Robinson includes:

Sept.	ffor ironwork for ye windows looking under ye roofe of ye South side Isle west of ye Dome, wt. 9c 00qr 13lb at 5d	21.05.05

Account to Thomas Coalburne, smith, includes:

	ffor iron work for 4 windows looking under ye roofe of ye South side Isle West of ye Dome, wt. 8c 2qr 3lb at 5d p.	19.17.11

Charges—October, 1699, to last day of September, 1700.

Jan. 1, 1699, to Mar. 31, 1700	To John Tijoue, Smith, ffor 8 new windows, wt. 147c 1qr 5lb at 6d p. lb.	412.08.06
	ffor 8 scrowls for ye top of the windows with a large moulding at £5 each	40.00.00
	ffor 364 foot of ornaments in ye double barrs of ye same windows at 4s p. foot	72.16.00
		£525.04.06

This item is not receipted.

NOTE.—In the account, Jan. 1 in each year is as above, instead of, as we should now write it, Jan. 1, 1700.

* In account for £85 5s. 4d. to Thomas Coalburne appears item:

April	ffor iron work for 4 windows, wt. 25c 1qr 2lb at 6d p. lb.	70.15.00

* In account for £41 0s. 7d. to Thomas Robinson appear items:

	ffor 40 cast iron windows to the Dome at 7s each	14.00.00
	ffor iron work for two windows in the roome over the north west vestry, wt. 2c 3qr 20lb at 5d p. lb ..	06.16.08

* In an account for £42 8s. 7d. to Thomas Coalburne appears:

	ffor 16 Stay barrs for the Dome very well worked double with Rings and Collars, wt. 20c 00qr 6lb at 4d p. lb.	37.08.08

* In an account of £128 0s. 9d. to Thomas Robinson appears:

	For ironwork for 4 large windows vizt. west north west, east and north east windows, wt. 26c 2lb at 5d p. lb.	60.14.02
	For 16 very large stay barrs well wrought with double iron and 32 rings for the Dome, wt. 19c. 0. 23lb. at 4 p. lb.	35.17.00
	To Sir Christopher Wren ffor his Expences in large Imperiall paper, pencills, Letters and postege, from Midsomer in the yeare 1675 to Michmas 1700, being 25 years and a quarter at £8 per annum.. ..	200.00.00

In account to Coalburne of £20 18s. 1d.:

Jan. 1 to Mar. 31, 1701.	For ironwork for six windows over the North East and North West vestries, wt. 8c 00qr 3lb. at 5d p. lb.	18.14.07

June 24th, 1701, to June 24th, 1702.

* Account to Thomas Coalburne for £15 17s. 2½d.:

Oct., 1701	For ironwork for two windows over the north east vestry, wt. 3c 00qr 22lb at 5d	07.09.02

*Not receipted.

* In account to Thomas Coalburne for £85 6s. 9½d. :

Jan., 1702 For 24 Barrs to 12 Windows in the Dome wrought to the circle of the Dome, each being 12 foot long, by 3 inches by 1½, with large square rings, to link the Chain, being welded and wrought well together, by two strong Spanish Barrs to bring them to the aforesaid scantling, wt. 36c 00qr 11lb. at 5d per lb. 84.04.07

* In account to Thomas Robinson for £79 1s. 3d. :

For 23 Barrs to 12 Windows wrought to the circle of the Dome, each 12 foot long, 3 inches by 1 inch and ½ with square rings to link the said chaine being welded and wrought well together by two substantial Spanish Barrs to bring it to the aforsaid scantling, wt. 32c 3qr 27lb at 5d p. lb. 76.19.07

* In account to Thomas Robinson for £253 17s. 11d. :

May, 1702 To Thomas Robinson, Smith, for iron work for 12 windows for the first order of the Dome, wt. 5 Tun 5c 0qr 16lb at 5d p. lb. 245.06.08

*In account to Thomas Coalburne for £252 10s. 11¼d.:

June, 1702 To Thomas Coalburne, Smith, For 12 windows for the First Ordor of the Dome, wt. 5Tun 5c 1qr 23lb. at 5d p. lb. 246.01.03

Oct. * To Thomas Coalburne, Smith, For 396 foot of Ornament, Balls, Screws and pinns in the 12 windows in the Dome, at 12d per foot running .. 19.16.00

For 2 half round headed windows in the Library and South side of the Church, wt. 5c 3qr 9lb at 5d per lb. 13.12.01

For 4 streight windows under the roofe of the south side Isle at the west end, wt. 9c 3qr 9lb at 5d per lb. 22.18.09

For 3 Casements and Frames for the said windows, wt. 1c 1qr 23lb. at 8d per lb 05.08.09

An exactly similar entry to the above follows to Thomas Robinson, save that he did three half round headed windows in library and over *east* end of church and "4 straight" windows on the *north* side.

Dec. To Thomas Robinson, Smith, for 3 large outside windows for the Library on ye North West end of the Church. wt. 29c 2qr 25lb at 5d p. lb. .. 69.07.01

For 87 foot running of ornament in ye same at 3s. 6d. per foot 15.04.06

*Not receipted.

For 4 windows 3 foot 9 inches high and 2 foot 7 in. broad with scrowles and other ornaments for the north and south, wt. 7c 1qr 25lb at 12d per lb... .. .. 41.17.00

126.08.07

February, 1703.—Exactly similar item to above appears to Thomas Coalburne for three windows to L on *south*.

Item in account to Thomas Coalburne for £23 1s. 9¾d.:

April For 3 new Casements and Frames for the windows of the South Library, wt. 3c 00qr 16lb at 8d per lb. .. 11.14.08

Item in account to Thomas Robinson on north side:

To Sr. Christopher Wren for ye value disbursed by him for Engraving ye following Designes, Views and Descriptions of this Fabric, vizt. Ground Plot, North prospect, East and West prospects (on the same plate), A large Section in perspective from East to West £225.00.00

For Copper plates 7.05

232.05.00

In account to Thomas Coalburne for £118 13s. 10d. :

Dec. For 3 windows to the Middle Isle, wt. 45c 2qr 19lb at 5d. 106.11.03

Ditto to T.R. for 3 *large* windows .. 95.17.01

May, 1704 To Thomas Coalburne, Smith, for work done by him in this month and March last . . . [and then follow details] 286.14.04¼

To Thomas Robinson, Smith, for work done by him in this month and January, February and March last. . . . [and then follow similar details to Thomas Coalburne] .. 306.08.07½

In account to Thomas Robinson for £95 11s. :

July, 1704 For a Rayle with Scrowles for the North East Arch under the Dome, wt. 19c 3qr 6lb at 10d p. lb., being 27½ foot run £92.07.06

Sept. To Thomas Coalburne, Smith, for a Balcony for one of ye Diagonall Arches in ye Dome, wt. 19c 3qr 7lb at 10d p. lb. 92.09.02

October To Thomas Coalburne, Smith, for a Balcony for one of the Diagonall Arches under the Dome, wt. 20c 2.13 at 10d p. lb. 96.04.02

In account to Thomas Robinson for £101 13s. 7½d. :

November For a Raile for ye Arch of the North West Corner of the Dome, wt. 19c. 3.5 at 10d p. lb. 92.07.06

In account to Thomas Robinson for £24 11s.:

Jan., 1705	For Rail in sevll. parts wth. Joynts for ye south stairs going up to the top of ye Dome, wt. 3.2.24 at 6d pr. lb...	10.00.00
	For 4 brases (?) for ye balconys of ye North East and West corners of ye Dome, wt. 4c 3qr 0 at 6d pr. lb.	13.06.00
March	To Thomas Robinson, Smith, for a large Window for ye North side next ye Library, wt. 16c 0qr 25lb at 5d pr. lb...	37.17.01
June	To John Tijoue, Smith, for ye fine Iron work of the Gates of ye two side Isles of ye Choire, by agreement for Iron, Workmanship and putting up	540.00.00

In account to Thomas Robinson for £131 11s. 11d.:

	For two half round Windows for ye West End, wt. 11c 1qr 20lb at 6d	£32.00.00
	For 45 fot. run of ornamt. to ye same windows at 12d p. fot.	02.05.00
	For 4 straight headed windows for ye North West Tower, wt. 22c 2qr 17lb. at 6d per lb	63.00.06

In account to Thomas Robinson for £189 5s. 2¼d.:

July	For 23 pieces of Railing for Mr. Rawlins Staircase, wt. 4c 3qr 22lb 6d. per lb.	13.17.00
	For a Window for the midle Isle at the West end, wt. 16c 2qrs 7lb at 5d p. lb.	38.12.11
	For 2 Windws, for ye West End, wt. 13c 1 qr 2lb at 5d p. lb.	30.19. 2
	For 2 Windows in Mr. Kempster's Tower, wt. 21c 1qr 2lb at 5d p. lb.	49.12. 6

In account to Thomas Robinson for £79 7s. 8¼d.:

September	To a large window for ye West End, wt. 18c 2 qr 13lb at 5d p. lb. ..	43. 8. 9
	For 2 oval Windows for ye South West Tower, wt. 0c 2qr 18lb at 5d p. lb.	1.10.10
March, 1706	To John Tijou, Smith, for the great Iron chain or Girdle round the Dome by Agreement for Iron and Workmanship (vizt.)	

	c	qr	lb	
Weight of said Chain	95	3	23	
Wedges	3	1	9	
	99	1	4	at 5½d p lb. 254.16. 8

For Extraordinary Workmanship in the Joynts	20. 0. 0
	274.16. 8

Note.—Robinson and Coalburne made the chains for the other domes and all straps, bolts, etc., for roofs.

June	To John Tijoue, Smith, for the Iron work of the round staircase in the South West Tower (vezt.) For 139½ of Rail and pannelling to ye staircase, and windows at 22s. 6d per foot	156.18. 9
	For 81½ foot of Iron work in the Hatch door and other ornamts. at the bottom of ye stairs at 36s p. foot	146.14.
		303.12. 9

In account to Thomas Robinson for £204 6s. 8½d.:

	To Thomas Robinson, Smith, for an Iron rail to stand before ye Consistory, wt. 22c 2qr 21lb at 9½d p. lb.	100.11. 7
	For a large Gerdle for ye Dome, wt. 45 c 2 qr 27lb at 4½d p. lb... ..	96. 1. 1½

In account to Thomas Robinson for £77 3s. 11½d.:

August	For 4 men a day each to put up window made by Mr. Colborn ..	0.10.0
September	Ditto but for 3 men	7.6
Nov.	Ditto—4 men, 2½ days	1. 5.0

No mention of its being for Coalburne.
Note.—Men's wage 2/6 per day.

In account to Thomas Robinson for £100 11s. 6¾d.:

Dec.	For new scrowl window and frame for ye west end under ye Pedamt., wt. 4c 1qr 17lb at 10d p. lb. ..	20.10.10
	For Windows vizt. 4 of ym. upright 2 oval and two halfround headed, wt. 27c 0 18lb at 5d p. lb.	63. 7. 6

In account to Thomas Robinson for £115 18s. 8½d.:

March, 1707	For Hinges with Squares, Joynts and plates Gudjeons all the eyes being Drilled, for ye great West N. and South Gates, 18c 2qr 10lb at 10½..	91. 1. 9

Under Taske worke—

June	To John Tijoue for fine Iron work vizt. In ye Balcony in ye wst. End 135 fot. ring of pannells at 2c 4qr.	297.0
	15 ft. 5 pillasters. 7.9.	111.15
		408.15
	For ye Altar Raile by agreement ..	260.0
		668.15

Up to p. 165, Vol. WB. 42.

From account to Thomas Robinson of £151 16s.:

July — To Thos. Robinson, Smith, for sundry Chains for ye Dome and Towers, wt. 26c 2qr 16lb at 4d p. lb. 49.14. 8

For a large chain and in addition to it for ye Dome, wt. 34c 1qr 17lb at $4\frac{1}{2}$d p. lb. .. .. 72. 4.$10\frac{1}{2}$

From account to Thomas Robinson for £178 11s. 6d.:

Sept. — For ironwork for ye Hands of ye Clock, 3c 1qr 12lb at 5d 7.16. 8

In account to Thomas Robinson for further amounts:

Oct. — 33 Rings for a chain for the Dome, 5cwt 2qr 4lb at 4d p. lb. 10. 6. 8

For a chain in ye Dome 22c 1qr 6lb at 4d p. lb. 41.12. 8

For altering 48 uprights for ye windows of the Dome at 4s. each .. 9.12. 0

For a chain for ye N.W. Tower, 10c 3qr 13lb at 4d p. lb. 20. 5. 8

In account to Thomas Robinson for £67 4s. 3d.:

Nov. — for a chain turned wth. a sweep for ye N. Tower, 4c 2qr 5lb at $4\frac{1}{2}$d .. 9.10.10

In account to Thomas Robinson for £45 0s. 1d.:

Dec. — For a compass chaine, wt. 10c 0qr 1lb at 4d. 18.13. 8

In account to Thomas Robinson for £53 18s. $6\frac{1}{4}$d.:

Jan., 1708 — For 6 Crosses for ye hands of ye Dyals, 12c 1qr at 6d... .. .. 34. 6. 0

In account to Thomas Robinson for £94 19s. $5\frac{1}{4}$d.:

April — for sundry chains for ye Dome, wt. 19c 3qr 2lb at 4d p. lb. .. .. 36.18.

In account to Thomas Robinson for £88 2s.:

May — For a Raile for stairs by ye S. Library, 1c 0qr 27lb. at 4d. 2. 6. 4

In account to Thomas Robinson for £64 16s. $7\frac{1}{4}$d.:

June — For a chain for Dome, 10c 3qr 2lb at 4d 20. 2. 0

For a Round Balcony for the great Cap inside the Dome, wt. 9c 2qr 21lb at 4d p. lb. 18. 1. 8

To Jane Brewen, Founder, for 144 Brass heads for ye Gt. Dores at 3s. a pair .. .. 21.12.

To John Tijoue for the Copper worke for the north West Tower vizt.

	c	*qr*	*lb*	
4 Scrolls qt. in Gross	10	3	27	
Ded. for Iron work in Do.	2	3	20	
Rems. at 3s p. lb.	8	0	7	135. 9.
Mold plinth and neck to the pine Great plinth to the Scroles and the pine qt. in Gross	6	3	0	
Ded. for Iron work in the Body of ye Scrolls ..	1	1	4	
Rems. at 4d p. lb. ..	5	1	24	122. 8.
Iron Work including Screws, 4c.0.24 at 9d p. lb.				17.14.
				275.11.

In account to Thomas Robinson for £209 3s. 6d.:

July, 1708 — for 24 Strong Iron rim Locks wth. Keys, Screws and nutts at 18s. each 21.12.

For 252 screws for ye Ironworke of ye Gt. Dores at 12d each .. .. 12.12.

From account to Thomas Robinson for £338 15s. 2d.:

Sept. — To Thomas Robinson, Smith, for a Round Balcony for ye Lantern cont. 8 pannels wth. Scroles open pillasters 4 balls and 8 plain pannells wth. bottom and top rail, wt. 85c 0qr 12lb at 7d per lb. 278. 0. 4

For Cast balls for ye same 2.2.16 at 4d. 4.18. 8

For Cramp .. .. 5.0.24 at $3\frac{3}{4}$d... .. .. 9. 2. 6

For a Chaine for ye Lanthorn, 5c 2qr 23lb at 4d 28.17. 0

In account to Thomas Robinson for £326 5s. 7d.:

Oct. — For 8 Windows for ye Dome the barrs being Circular, wt. 20c 3qr 10lb at 6d. .. .. 58. 7.

Nov. — To Thomas Robinson, Smith, for 14 hoops, Crosses, and Staples wth. sevll. sorts of Iron worke and much square frames and abundance of screws wt. together 24c 1qr with screwing and many alterations at 12d p. lb. .. .. 135.16.

In the margin, written in a different hand, are the words "Ball and Cross." There is a half-inch scale drawing of the Ball and Cross dated June 29th, 1708, at bottom and April 26th, 1708, at top.

In account to Thomas Robinson for £141 18s. 7d.:

	For 3 large Brass Locks and Keys and 3 polisht Bolts wth. plates, Screws, Staples &c for ye Gt. Dores of ye Library	10. 0. 0

December.—Account to Thomas Robinson for £102 1s. for various matters.

From account to Thomas Robinson for £81 0s. 4d.:

Jan., 1709	For 7 large Locks for ye Gt. Dores at £6 each	42.00.
	For 15 Brass Escocheons and Screws for Do. 15s each	11. 5
	For ye Pattern and repairing it ..	0.15

From account to Thomas Robinson for £33 7s. 9d.:

Feb.	For 3 large Brass Locks wth. Keys &c for ye Library	5. 5
	For 3 pair of polisht Bolts on Brass plates for Do.	4.10
	For a new Lock and 3 Keys for ye Geometry stairs	3.10. 0
	For a Brass Escotcheon and screws to Do.	0.15. 0

Further account for odds and ends to Thomas Robinson: March, £18 4s. 4½d.; April, £20 15s. 8d.; May, £30 16s. 2d.; June, £7 3s. 9d.; July, £20 4s. 5d.

From account to Thomas Robinson for £138 6s. 7d.:

August	For 46 Steps for ye South West Tower going up to ye Clockweights, wt. 45c 2qr 27lb at 5d p. lb. ..	106.14. 7

From account to Thomas Robinson for £83 16s. 2d.:

Sept.	For 5 Grates for ye paving being under the brasses in ye angles and center of ye Dome, wt. 5c 3qr 03lb at 2s p. lb.	64.14. 0

Accounts to Thomas Robinson, sundries: October, £63 0s. 2½d.; November, £75 0s. 2d.

	To Andrew Niblett, Copper smith, for 5 brass plates and planished and polished for the Dome, the middle one wch. is 4f. Diamr. and a half inch thick and the other 4 wch. are 2 fot. Diamr. is ¼ and ½ thick all the sd. 5 plates, wt. 5c 3qr 3¼lb. at 3s p. lb.	97. 1. 9
	For Drilling and fileing 2064 holes in the same plates at 12d each ..	103. 4. 0
	paid the Engraver for graving the same	7.12. 0
	For putting on the sd. plates to the Iron frames and making the holes being 32 in number wider for the brass screws to come through wth. Screws and screwing ye same and other workmanship	4. 0. 0

December.—Account to Thomas Robinson, sundries £99 1s. 5d.:

Morning Prayer Chappell
For 616 fot. of supll. wainscott flooring and stepps . . .

January, 1710.—Account to Thomas Robinson, sundries, £75 16s. 3d.

From account to Thomas Robinson for £109 7s. 6d.:

Feb.	For 8 Casemts. and frames for ye 2 Towers, wt. 8c 2qr 22lb at 8d p. lb.	32. 9. 4

From account to Thomas Robinson for £152 14s.:

March	For loan of the Stillyard to weigh the great Bell wth. his own and men's attendce.	10.15.

From account to Thomas Robinson for £108 11s. 7d.:

April	For 26 windows for the Newell of the great stairs, wt. 15c 1qr 26lb at 5d p. lb.	36. 2. 6

From account to Thomas Robinson for £49 13s. 7d.:

May	For 4 men 3 days each setting up and cleaning the Gates to ye Isles going to ye Choire	1. 8. 0
	For a pannell for a Balcony in the Dome, wt. 5c 3qr 14lb at 6d p. lb.	16. 9. 0

From account to Thomas Robinson for £127 9s. 3d. Last item is:

June	For 2 sets of railing wth. Scroles and Spikes and fluted Collumns for the steps at the W.End, wt. 38c 3qr 16lb at 6d p. lb. by agreement	108.18. 0

Book WB43 stops at this, with a good quarter of the book remaining blank.

Book WB 44 starts June 24th, 1714. Each page is now headed "From 24th June, 1714 to 31st Dec. following inclusive."

In account to Thomas Robinson for £95 4s. 8d. for "repairs":

	the two Iron Gates and Wickets and spikes on the South side of the Church	85.00.00

Account to Thomas Robinson—

	ffor worke done at the Chapter House—small items	83.18.06

June 24, 1714, to Dec. 31, 1714. To Richard Jones, Smith, ffor the Large Iron ffence round the Church vizt.—

For Gates ..	12
Large Ballesters	149
Small do. ..	2516
Scrowles	157
Railes	314
Spikes	5051
Baces for do. ..	2422
Stubs & baces ..	8
Plates for Scrowles	146
Stubs & Steps for the Gates to hang on & shutt against ..	31
Bolts for the Breaks & Piers	194
Steeled Punches	6
Small Plates, pins & wedges.	

	Tun c q lb.	
Totall wt. at 6d p. lb.	207.5.3.09	£11608.06.06
Deducted from sev'll Parcells return'd	7.5.0.12	406.06.00
Rems. for acco't at 6d p. lb. ..	200.0.2.25	11202.00.06

Account to Thomas Robinson:

31 Dec., 1714, to 24 June, 1715.	Sundries	28.12.5

From account to Benjamin Mawson, smith:

31 Dec., 1718, to 24 June, 1719.	For 8 Copper Astricks, 2 long Cornishes and twelve short—16.3.18 at 2s. 6d.	236.15.00
	For 17 pieces of Copper Cornish and eight Copper Astricks for the West Diall—16.2.27 at 2/6 ..	234.07.06

CHAPTER VI

THE WELSH SMITHS

THE study of wrought ironwork is frequently made the more enjoyable by the fact that the field open to the smith of the early eighteenth century was usually confined within the radius of a few miles of his forge. In several instances it is possible to see practically all the best work of one man in a long day, and so to obtain an insight into his likes, dislikes, merits and failures which might otherwise remain unrecognised. One of the most interesting examples of these clustered groups is to be found in North Wales, in a series of screens and gates in and around the neighbourhood of Wrexham. Hitherto this work has been ascribed by tradition to the "Roberts Brothers of Chirk," whose name must now be altered to the

119.—GATES AND SCREEN, WREXHAM PARISH CHURCH.

120.—GATES AND SCREEN, ST. PETER'S CHURCH, RUTHIN.

121.—DETAIL, GATES, CHIRK CASTLE (FIG. 124).

122.—GATE, OSWESTRY PARISH CHURCH.

brothers Robert and John Davies of Groes Voyle, Bersham, North Wales, who flourished between 1702 and 1755.

To the striking gates of Chirk Castle belongs the equally striking legend that the gates were the work of a local smith named Roberts and his daughter! This tradition of a female element in their production is persistent, although sometimes she is said to have been a sister. More generally it is held that the gates were by two brothers Roberts, and it used to be so stated in the local guide to the castle. Had any doubt existed on the point, it should have been set at

123.—PARISH CHURCH GATES, OSWESTRY.

rest by the following statement in Mr. Starkie Gardner's book, *English Ironwork of the Seventeenth and Eighteenth Centuries*, in which he says:

> For the name of these smiths we are indebted to Mr. Myddelton, the owner of the ancient castle of Chirk, near Llangollen, who has ascertained from his family accounts that his gates were made for Sir Robert Myddelton, by two brothers, local smiths named Roberts, for the price of £190 1s. 6d.

In view of the evidence we now possess, it is difficult to see how such a mistake can have been made. There is little doubt, however, that in making the statement Mr. Myddelton relied upon

124.—THE ENTRANCE GATES, CHIRK CASTLE.

125.—THE WHITE GATES AND SCREEN, LEESWOOD HALL, MOLD.

126.—THE WHITE GATES, LEESWOOD HALL, MOLD.

his memory, and in so doing gave his information unconsciously in such a form as to make it appear irrefutable. It is curious to see how far-reaching may be the effect of such an error. Mr. Gardner, accepting the information, based upon it his history of the group of ironwork in the locality, and ascribed it all to the same brothers Roberts. It must be added that, where

127.—THE BLACK GATES, LEESWOOD HALL, MOLD.

evidence has been forthcoming, he was right in ascribing it to the same smiths, though the name was not Roberts.

A search for the actual date and cost of the beautiful screen in the churchyard of Wrexham Parish Church led to the discovery (through the kindness of Mr. Neobard Palmer of Wrexham) of the following entry in the churchwardens' register for 1719–23 :

2 June 1720 Pd William Rogers for taking down the old gate Robert Davies Smith paid £24

This was quickly followed by the receipt of invaluable extracts from the few remaining pages of the original disbursement books of Robert Myddelton, Esq., of Chirk Castle, 1718–33. For these we owe a deep debt of gratitude to Mr. W. M. Myddelton of

128.—THE SCREEN, EATON HALL, CHESHIRE.

Lincoln, who has been untiring in placing information at our disposal. The entries run as follows :

1719 July 28 Smiths Iron Gates	Pd Robert Davies, Smith in full of what he and his Brother did at ye Iron Gates from ye 14 Octob 1717 to ye 21 December following	10. 16. 9
1721 Aug 15	Pd Mr. Robert Davies, Smith ye remaind[r] of all due to him and his Brother John for workeing ye Iron Gates before ye ffront of ye Castle	12. 13. 06

And again on September 15th of the same year is a quaintly worded entry :

being a mistake in ye last payment made ye 15 Aug and he under pd by.. .. .. 1. 13. 6

So much for the makers of the great gates at Chirk Castle. But these entries by no means complete the chain of evidence afforded by these loose sheets, for reference will presently be made to entries of payments made to Robert Davies for the Wrexham churchyard gates already mentioned and for the gates at Ruthin Church. But, for the moment, the Chirk gates may be examined briefly, as they are notable in several respects. Pre-eminently the work of an

129.—GATES AT ERDDIG PARK, WREXHAM.

130.—AT ERDDIG PARK, WREXHAM.

uneducated mind, they show an entire lack of constructive design and of a sense of proportion; but while the whole scheme is incongruous to a degree, yet there is a certain barbaric splendour about it. Their chief interest lies in the great gate piers, largely on account of the massive cast-iron caps and bases, which, with the exception, perhaps, of the old cast-iron firebacks of Sussex, must be almost the earliest ornamental cast ironwork in the country. The circular moulded balusters, too, appear to be cast iron and are a characteristic feature of the Davies' work. They enclose the not less unusual and crudely naturalistic vines which grow spirally from ornamental pots standing on the bases of the piers. The gates themselves are so violently out of scale, with the sprawling overthrows and side panels, as to make them appear more fussy than they really are. The fixed side wings (pardonably mistaken by Mr. Gardner for wickets) form by far the most commendable portion of the design, and, with the exception of the branching sprigs of bay leaves to the crestings, they are daintily designed, and may be taken as good examples of the Davies' work. The brothers were invariably happier in their results when they avoided grandiose schemes that led them into regions of design beyond their powers. The lead wolves surmounting the gate piers represent the cognisance of the Myddelton family, who claim their descent from Ririd Flaidd (Young Wolf) in the paternal line, and, in the maternal line, Blaidd Rhudd (Red Wolf), the coat of arms being "three wolves' heads erased."

For the Wrexham gates, in the same accounts of Robert Myddelton occurs the following entry :

1720 Oct. 7. Pd. Robert Davies, Smith 10 li wch my master subscrib'd towards ye Iron Gates at Wrexham Church yard .. .. 10. 0. 0.

The churchwardens' registers for 1719–23 were lost for some years, recovered and lost again ! Happily, they have once again been returned through the efforts of Mr. George Frater of Wrexham, but no opportunity has since occurred of examining them. It is reported, however, that they contain no further reference to the gates than that already given. The chancel gates,

131.—SMALL GATES, EMRAL HALL, NEAR BANGOR, FLINTSHIRE.

which have already been referred to in Chapter II, are possibly the work of Robert Davies' father, Hugh Davies, whose burial is recorded in the Wrexham parish register, September 2nd, 1702.

This Hugh Davies of Groes Voyle, Bersham, near Wrexham, by his will dated June 13th, 1702, left his messuage in Bersham, with appurtenances, to his wife Eleanor and then to his son Robert, and also a sum of £7 10s., " for which he is to instruct my son Thomas in the trade and science of a smith." His sons Hugh and John, as well as six daughters, are also mentioned. The brothers are alleged to have worked later on under Tijou at Drayton House,

132.—MAIN GATES, EMRAL HALL, NEAR BANGOR, FLINTSHIRE.

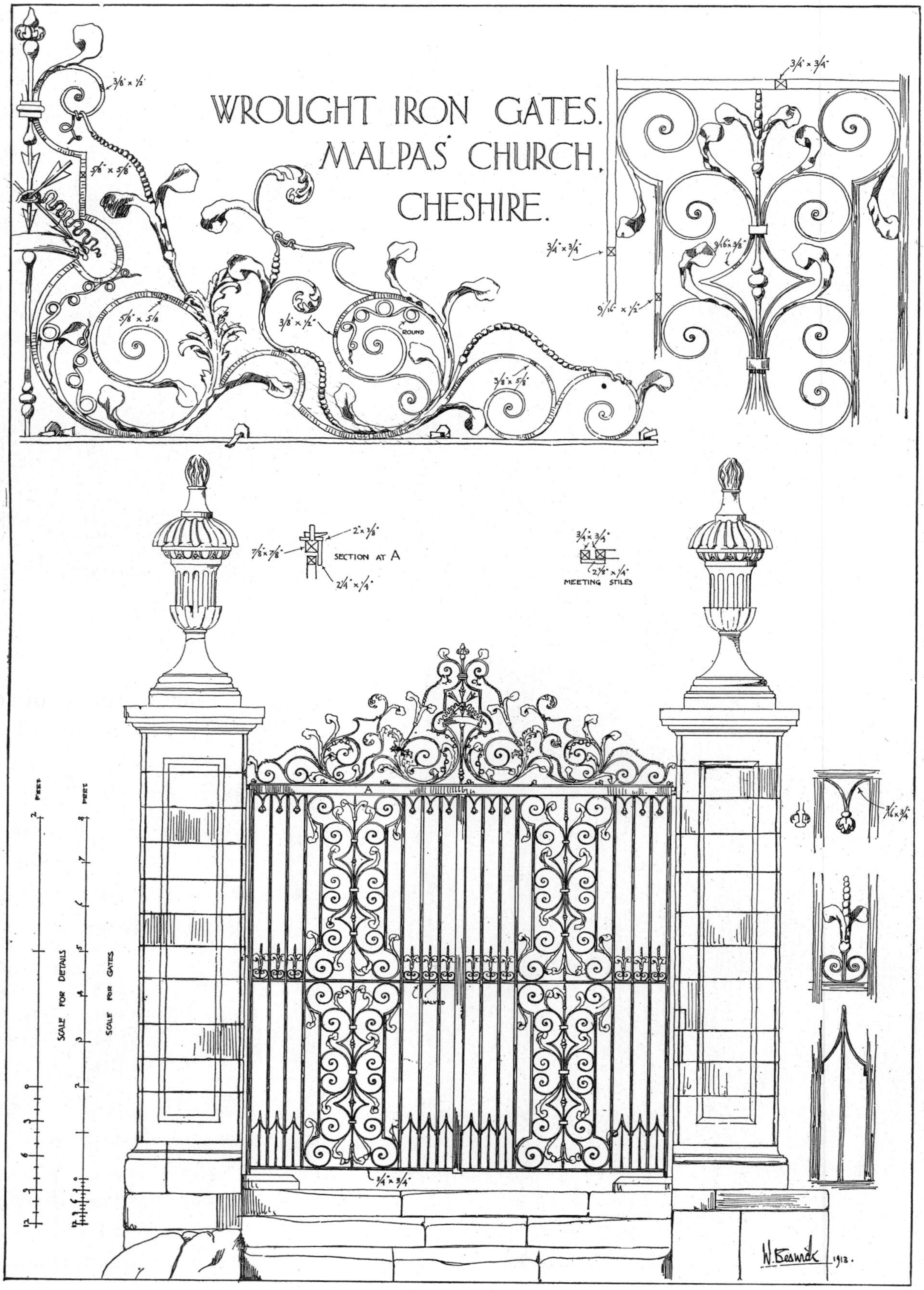

133.—DRAWING AND DETAILS OF GATES, MALPAS CHURCH, CHESHIRE.

and they may also have worked for Bakewell, for they sometimes use features typical of his designs, such as the openwork shell at Newnham Paddox.

We will now leave Wrexham for the gates of St. Peter's Church, Ruthin, some few miles distant. The following entries appear in the accounts of Robert Myddelton :

1727. Jan. 22. Pd. Robert Davies of Croes Voel, Smith which my master was pleased to give towards erecting Iron Gates upon Ruthin Church yard, Mr. Watt Williams and other Subscribers' money was pd. ye sd smith 20li in pte for the said Gates ye same day .. .. .. 5. 5. 0.

There are also several entries concerning the gates in the churchwardens' accounts on various dates during the years 1728–31. These the Rev. Lewis Pryce, the Warden of Ruthin, has kindly furnished. The wording of the first (April 10th, 1728) is of interest. It records that Edward Price of Llanbedr " contributes 10s. 6d. towards making ye new gate," and so confirms the date of their manufacture. This might otherwise be left open to doubt by an earlier entry in the Myddelton accounts dated November 2nd, 1720, which runs :

Pd. by Mr. Roberts to Robert Davies, Smith for ye Iron work done at Ruthin Church .. 23. 18. 1.

It is not at all clear to what ironwork this refers. It is unlikely that the gates were made eight years before they were erected, nor would Mr. Myddelton have subscribed so odd a sum in part payment of them.

The gates are very characteristic of the Davies' work, light in construction, with a clever handling of open scrollwork, disfigured by the presence of one or two ill-considered details

134.—DOUBLE GATES, MALPAS CHURCH, CHESHIRE.

135.—SINGLE GATE, MALPAS CHURCH, CHESHIRE.

which might, with a little thought, have been corrected. In the wicket gates, for instance, what could be more unpleasant than breaking the back of the scrolls to follow the line of the hanging bar at the top hinge? The caps to the piers are delightful; the use of the little circular moulded pillars and cut pelmet above the abacus is a happy and original treatment. The husk festoons falling on either side of the cherub in the overthrow are direct copies on a small scale of Tijou's festoons in the Fountain Garden screen at Hampton Court.

136.—PORCH GATES, MALPAS CHURCH, CHESHIRE.

At Oswestry we are once more lucky in finding actual accounts, though the gates themselves are not of the same quality as those already mentioned, the centre panels of the double gates and the general lines of the overthrow being poor. The churchwardens' book for the lower division of the parish contains the following:

> The Disburstments of John Kynaston one of the Churchwardens of the Parish of Oswestry in the year 1738 Lower Division—
> For Mr. Davies my part for the Iron Gates 11. 10. 4.

The parish registers also show that the total cost of the gates was £31 11s.—which was to be met in equal third shares by the town and the upper and lower divisions of the parish—and record the payment of this sum to "Mr. Davies of Cross Voyle." From this it would appear that the lower division paid £1 more than their fair share!

The most important example of the other work, which is the great screen or "White Gates" at Leeswood Hall, Mold, a few miles from Wrexham and Ruthin, is a truly wonderful piece of work and one of the finest screens in the country. The detail is good throughout, and the whole effect would have been magnificent if a plain horizontal line between the piers had been kept instead of the series of broken pediments. These have the effect of reducing the length of the screen, which is actually 100ft., while the height is about 17ft. to the apex of the pediments.

On the high road to Mold, a mile or so away, are the "Black Gates," which have always been used as the entrance to the park. Twenty feet to the top of the overthrow, they are a remarkably fine production. While very different in character from the White Gates ("Heaven" and "Hell" they are known as locally), there are several details common to both. One peculiarity in particular must be pointed out, as it occurs again in the well known screen at Eaton Hall, Chester, and is the best evidence that we have at present that the latter screen is also the work of the Davies. This is the presence of the curious diamond fret patterns in the piers of all three and in the friezes of the Eaton and of the Leeswood screens. It is difficult to reconcile the really fine powers of design exhibited in these gates with the uneducated production at Chirk Castle ; but time and experience work wonders, and the twenty years that may well have passed between the making of the latter in 1719 and the erection of the Eaton and Leeswood screens may account for this difference.

The hall at Eaton, Chester, as shown in a print by Badeslade of about 1740, is attributed to Vanbrugh, and for the design of the screen he may possibly have given the general lines, which are strikingly unusual. Here, again, are found the small circular moulded terminals at the four corners of the caps to the piers, already noticed in the caps at Ruthin and Wrexham. The design has been practically reproduced at Newnham Paddox, Leicestershire, and only differs in detail. A part of the latter has, however, been attributed to Bakewell, and closely resembles his work at Derby.

137.—ABBEY HOUSE GATES, SHREWSBURY.

At Erddig Hall, near Wrexham, the seat of Mr. Phillip Yorke, are gates and railings, the latter probably the richest example of wrought-iron railing existing in England. It was, so it is said, made originally for Stanstey Park, and was moved to its present position some few years ago. The design and workmanship leave little room for doubt that this, too, is the work of the Davies brothers. The spacing of the circular moulded supports to the bottom rail is curious, and is the more irritating as it is so entirely unnecessary. There is a fine swing about the great scrolls forming the cresting, which would, however, be better in proportion to a railing of twice this height.

At Emral Hall, near Bangor, Flintshire, some ten miles south-east of Wrexham, are two very interesting pairs of gates. A large pair between stone piers is seen in the distance in the illustration of the smaller gates, which are most unusual both in their form and dainty workmanship. The fact that they are very badly constructed must be admitted, but the design is, nevertheless, charming. Here, again, on a smaller scale, are caps almost identical with those at Ruthin. In an article upon Emral by Mr. Avray Tipping, which appeared in *Country Life* some years ago, the writer mentioned the existence of the original accounts for the new wings to the hall, dated 1724–27, but, in spite of every effort, they are not forthcoming: a thousand pities, for it is more than probable that they contain some reference to the ironwork. The typical tall and flimsy overthrow resembles that at Oswestry in its main lines, though it is more top-heavy, and it is not surprising to find that the former has more than once been blown over by the wind.

138.—GATES, CARDEN HALL, NEAR MALPAS, CHESHIRE.

And now we come to the beautiful gates to Malpas Churchyard—it must be confessed with some misgiving. Are they or are they not the work of the Davies brothers? One would like to think so, and yet one cannot help recognising, both in their workmanship and design, a far higher standard than that realised in any of the work previously described. Both the double and the single gates are gems in their way; there is much delicacy and feeling in their design, which is carried to completion with no loose ends or unforeseen difficulties hurriedly and awkwardly met. Robert Davies died in 1749, and his brother John in 1755, and in some respects the gates bear the stamp of some ten to fifteen years later than this latter date. There is little doubt that the

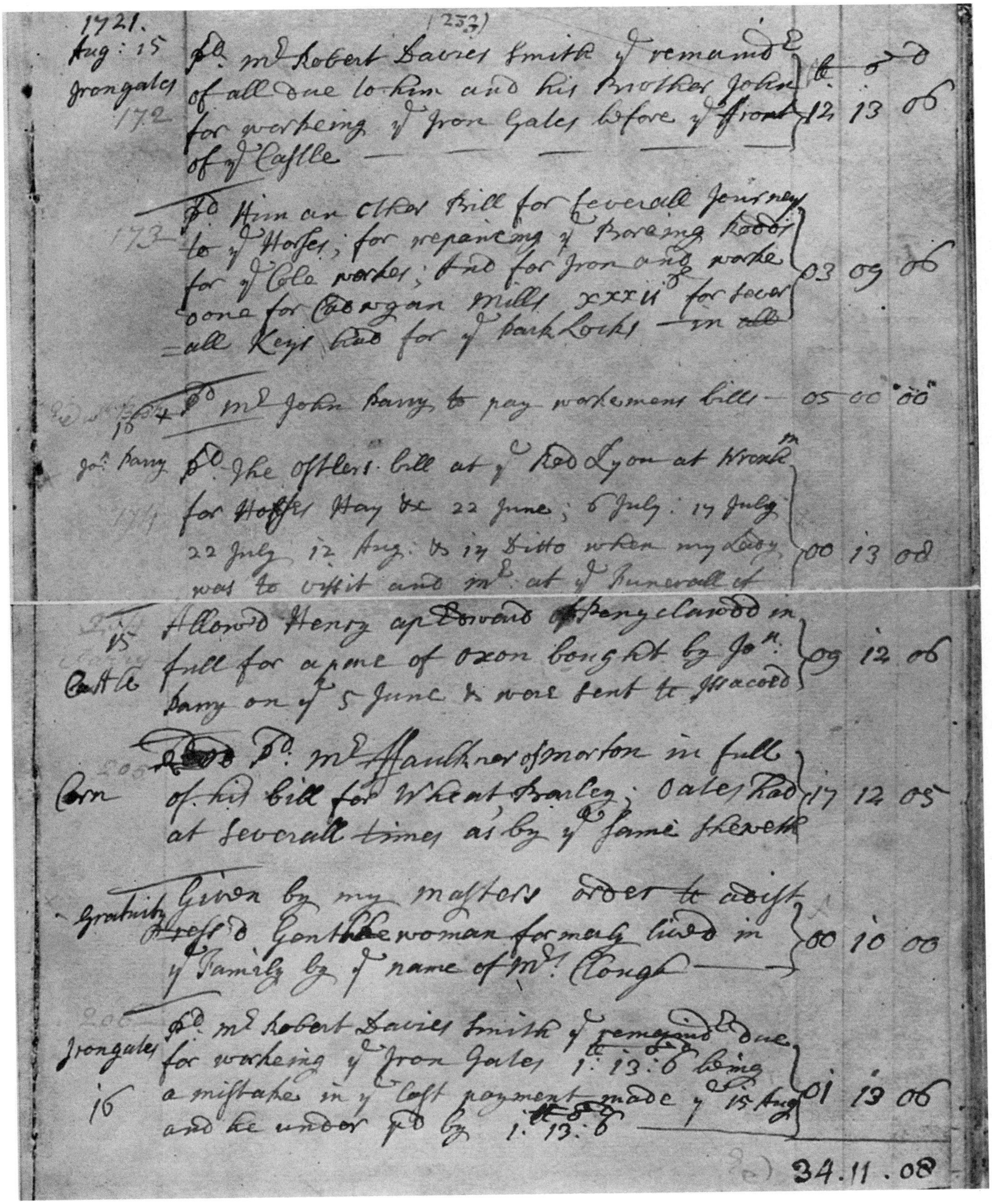

1721. Aug: 15 Irongates 172	Pd. Mr Robert Davies Smith ye remaindr of all due to him and his Brother John for working ye Iron Gates before ye front of ye Castle	12	13	06
173	Pd. Him an other Bill for Severall Journeys to ye Horses, for repairing ye Boreing Rodds for ye Cole works; and for Iron and worke done for Cadwgan Mills xxxii for Severall Keys had for ye back Locks	03	09	06
10	Pd. Mr John Barry to pay workemens bills	05	00	00
Jno. Barry	Pd. The Ostlers bill at ye Red Lyon at Wrexm for Horses Hay &c 22 June; 6 July. 17 July 22 July 12 Aug: & 17 Ditto when my Lady was to visit and Mr. at ye Funerall of	00	13	08
15 Cattle	Allowed Henry ap Edward of Penyclawdd in full for a paire of Oxen bought by Jno. Barry on ye 5 June & were sent to Ffacodd	09	12	06
Corn	Pd. Mr Ffaulkner of Morton in full of his bill for Wheat, Barley, Oates had at Severall times as by ye same sheweth	17	12	05
Gratuity	Given by my Masters order to assist a poor Gentlewoman formerly lived in ye Family by ye name of Mrs. Clough	00	10	00
Irongates 16	Pd. Mr Robert Davies Smith ye remainder due for working ye Iron Gates 1:13:6 being a mistake in ye last payment made ye 15 Aug and he under pd by 1:13:6	01	13	06
		34.	11.	08

139.—FACSIMILE REPRODUCTION OF EXTRACT FROM THE ORIGINAL DISBURSEMENT BOOK OF ROBERT MYDDELTON, ESQ., CHIRK CASTLE, 1718 TO 1733.

(By the courtesy of W. M. Myddelton, Esq.)

charming little gate between the retaining walls on either side of the path leading to the porch is of an earlier date than the others—it recalls the chancel gates in Wrexham Church. The pair of gates to the porch itself is interesting in that it is unusual to find iron gates in this position ; but they are poor indeed in comparison with the others. In connection with one's doubts about the work at Malpas, it may be mentioned that there is a gate in the kitchen garden at Eaton Hall which is reminiscent in design, as Mr. Starkie Gardner points out, of the work at St. Paul's

140.—GATES, POWIS CASTLE.

Cathedral and Hampton Court by Jean Tijou. It certainly has no resemblance to any of the work which we know to have been produced by the Davies brothers ; and it may be that this gate and those at Malpas were by some smith employed only casually in Cheshire.

Another design showing similar graceful scrollwork, with both flowing and broken scrolls, is seen in the gate at the Abbey House, Shrewsbury. This work is attributed to the Davies brothers, but the ascription is unsupported except as regards internal evidence.

The dog-bars are scrolled and spear-headed like those at Leeswood and other of the Davies' works. They are, however, not well managed in the flanking screens, where they seem squat in proportion and as if they had been intended for the gates and were afterwards cut down to fit the railing. The design, as a whole, however, is graceful and rather unusual, and exemplifies the later manner of these smiths.

In the magnificent, though florid, gates at Powis Castle, we find a great contrast with the Shrewsbury gates. The ironwork at the Castle is obviously in an earlier and cruder manner. It has much in common with the Chirk Castle gates and shows the same love for extravagant detail and (in the plate iron shells at either side especially) the same lack of a sense of scale. On the whole, however, it is more refined and strives less for effect, and, as it lacks sufficient of the hall-marks of the Davies' work, is at present ascribed only and not definitely classified as of their forging.

At Carden Hall, near Malpas, Cheshire, the gates and screen have also been attributed to the brothers, and, if theirs, must be counted as a late example. Points of resemblance to their other work can be seen in the light and flimsily constructed overthrow which recalls that at Emral, especially in some of the leafwork and the crowning feature of the side panels, and the overthrow at Ruthin, especially in the general form and the tall central post. The dog-bars, springing from scrolls, and the husks with twisted tongues are curious and unpleasing features of the railings.

Other work which has been attributed to the Davies brothers includes that at Plas Llanrydd and Mere Hall, near Droitwich ; but the before mentioned are the chief examples of their work.

CHAPTER VII

THE WEST OF ENGLAND SMITHS

BRISTOL was a port of considerable importance in the seventeenth and eighteenth centuries, and her prosperous merchant venturers found an outlet for their surplus profits in a civic generosity for which the city is still celebrated. It is to this circumstance, no doubt, that Bristol owes much of the magnificent wrought ironwork which, in the form of sword-rests, gates and screens, adorns her churches and public buildings.

In the days of these old adventurers it was the custom of the Lord Mayor, during his year of office, to visit not only his own parish church, but also one of the city churches, and this custom still prevails in Bristol and in Bath, and possibly other West Country towns. The great sword, which was borne aloft in the mayoral procession, was carried into the church and placed upright in full view of the congregation in an elaborate sword-rest. Surmounted by a crown and decorated with cut sheet-metal foliage or scrollwork, and gilded, these sword-rests are, perhaps, the most pleasing and unique relics of an age noted for its achievements in the field of wrought ironwork.

141.—GATES, ST. MARY REDCLIFF, BRISTOL.

Reference has already been made in Chapter IV to seventeenth century sword-rests in Bristol, and in this chapter we shall see that the early work was followed by an exceptionally fine series of sword-stands (as they are often called), grilles and gates

142.—GATE, ST. MARY REDCLIFF, BRISTOL.

143.—SCREEN, TEMPLE CHURCH, BRISTOL.

of the eighteenth century period. It is fortunate that, of the best examples of wrought ironwork found in Bristol, records exist which give the name of the smith, William Edney. Among these examples the gates at St. Mary Redcliff are outstanding. Entries for these gates appear in the churchwardens' accounts for 1710, and they show that payment of a sum of £110 was made for a pair of gates to divide the nave from the chancel. Taking this amount with the size of the gates, the payment works out at about one guinea per foot super, as compared with £2 per foot super charged by Tijou.

These gates are not now in their original position, but at the west end of the church, in the arch on the south side, and two side panels have been added to fill the arch opening. The gates are 9ft. in height and 7ft. 6ins. wide, including the pilasters but excluding the side panels, and the height from floor to overthrow is 14ft. The general design is exceptionally good, the lower panels of the gates being reminiscent of the gates to the garden front at Hampton Court, previously referred to. The overthrow is pyramidal in form, excellently filled with the coat of arms and crest of the city of Bristol.

144.—GATES, TEMPLE CHURCH, BRISTOL.

Two other gates, one on either side of the chancel, have an unusual form of dog-bar not found elsewhere, and the overthrow filling the pointed arch is also noteworthy and unusual. Indeed, the design of the whole is a very happy example of a sympathetic handling of the problem of providing suitable ironwork of Renaissance period to harmonise with architecture of a previous age. The width of the opening is 4ft. 1in. and the height to the springing is 8ft. A photograph of one of these gates is shown in Fig. 142.

Of the sword-rests, that in the Temple Church is only excelled by that at St. Nicholas', and is, therefore, one of the finest in existence. In its present state it measures 11ft. 3½ins. from the foot to the top of the crown, excluding the cross ; but the additional ironwork now fixed below the cup and attached to its flanking scrolls seems to be an afterthought, and the height of the original portion, from the foot of the central standard to the top of the cross, measures eight feet.

The design closely resembles the sword-rest in St. Nicholas' Church, though it differs in some points—for instance, the cup is not, in this case, a shell, but is formed in acanthus leaf. The fine beaked grotesques, which terminate in acanthus leaves, are in the manner of Tijou, and measure nearly two feet across.

The screens at Temple Church date from 1726, and they are said by some authorities to have been made by William Edney, from the evidence of one of the monograms which display the letters " W. E." The gates are not in their original position, and they now act as screens to divide the choir from the north and south aisles. Each bay is approximately 12ft. long, while the gates are 5ft. high and 4ft. 6ins. in width. The colour is black and is effective, but the silhouette is impaired by the lack of a suitable background.

In an excellent description of this ironwork in *Eighteenth Century Architecture of Bristol*, Mr. Dening says :

> The omission of a frieze between the lower and upper panels and the independent treatment of the adjoining standards is not an advance on the Redcliff model.
>
> Some of the acanthus leaf work, instead of emphasising the constructional lines, rather obliterates them by intruding upon adjoining members. Harts-tongue ferns (water-leaves) are freely used in conjunction with the acanthus. The lower panels are rather restless owing to the exuberance of scroll-work.
>
> The heads of these gates, like those at St. Nicholas', are shaped, the " S " scrolls in this instance effectively filling the spandrils.

While the name of the smith is not known, the workmanship is fine and may well be that of William Edney ; but the design cannot be compared with that of the gates at St. Mary Redcliff, the upper panels being noticeably lacking in constructional lines. But, as evidence against the suggestion that this is foreign work, the husks and the leaves springing from them at the top and bottom of the circular frame to the monogram panels and terminating abruptly at the central

145.—GATES, ST. NICHOLAS' CHURCH, BRISTOL.

146.—SWORD-REST, TEMPLE CHURCH, BRISTOL.

147.—SWORD-REST, ST. PAUL'S CHURCH, BRISTOL.

148.—SWORD-REST, ST. NICHOLAS', BRISTOL.

horizontal bar are similar to the husks and side leaves to the monogram panels of the gates in St. Nicholas' Church. The husks are also identical with those found in the upper panels of the Redcliff gates. Both from the evidence, therefore, of the initials "W. E." and from the evidence of the husks and leaves, it seems probable that Edney was the smith employed.

The gates at St. Nicholas' Church were probably made in the second decade of the eighteenth century, but were removed from the chancel in 1743, when they were widened by the addition of two narrow side panels to enable them to fit their present position, where they enclose the baptistery at the west end of the church. From the floor to the top of the urns surmounting the side panels the height is 7ft. 9ins. and the width 8ft.

Mr. Dening calls attention to an interesting feature thus : " The upper panels of the gates with their complicated monograms display the suspended features similar to those at Redcliff." These aptly described " suspended features," though lacking in constructional value, are peculiar to Edney's work and valuable as evidence of his handicraft. " The general lines of the design follow those of Redcliff, but acanthus scrolls are used more freely and the whole scheme is more boldly conceived. The cast urns with their drapery pendants are almost identical with those at Temple Church."

The finest example of an eighteenth century sword-rest existing is in St. Nicholas' Church (Fig. 148). It is 10ft. in height and 2ft. 4ins. at its greatest width. The central standard is 1in. square and the smaller bars are $\frac{3}{4}$in. by $\frac{1}{4}$in. The whole is enriched on both sides with free acanthus foliage, vigorous yet delicate in treatment, terminating beneath the ring in beaked grotesques, in the manner of Tijou. The ring carries the monogram of Queen Anne ; the scrolls above this have been mutilated, and probably acanthus enrichment is missing. A gilded crown terminates the design in the usual manner. This great rest is attached to the wall below the cup with one bar only, and is, therefore, constantly in a state of visible oscillation.

The sword-hilt rested in a cup, which, in this example, is in the form of a shell attached to

149.—GATES, REDLAND GREEN CHAPEL, BRISTOL.

150.—GATE, REDLAND COURT, BRISTOL.

the standard 2ft. 4ins. from the floor, and here, again, empty rivet holes in the bars indicate mutilation.

The central standard is reeded on the face in an unusual and delightful manner. This piece of work shows an exceptional refinement of detail, particularly in the diminishing thickness and perfect convolution of the scrolls. The lettering of the monogram, also, is one of the finest examples of smithcraft to be found in the country.

The only examples worthy to be classed with it are the well known examples in the Victoria and Albert Museum, South Kensington.

Before leaving the subject of sword-rests, and in contrast with the magnificent example in St. Nicholas', an illustration is here given (Fig. 147) showing the utter eclipse which overtook

151.—LAMP STANDARD AND TORCH EXTINGUISHER, ROYAL FORT HOUSE, BRISTOL.

152.—STAIRCASE BALUSTRADE, ROYAL FORT HOUSE, BRISTOL.

smithcraft in the late eighteenth and early nineteenth centuries. The sword-rest in St. Paul's Church, Portland Square, is a convincing proof that the decline of the arts had already begun well before the nineteenth century, for it dates from 1790 (Dening, *loc. cit.*).

At the Royal Fort (House), which is now the headquarters of the Department of Education, Bristol University, can be seen some excellent examples of the handicraft of West Country smiths. The balustrades to the steps and landing of the main entrance terminate in scrolled and buttressed

153.—GATES, ELMORE COURT, GLOUCESTERSHIRE.

154 and 155.—RAILINGS, ALBEMARLE ROW, BRISTOL.

lamp standards and torch-extinguishers of unusually graceful design (Fig. 151), excelling anything of the kind in the sister city of Bath, and worthy of comparison with the best types in London. In the staircase hall (Fig. 152) we have two arresting features which vie with each other for notice. Against a background of white plaster, attractively modelled in high relief with most naturalistic vines, is displayed an unusual wrought-iron balustrade, simple, graceful and altogether worthy of the earlier tradition.

At Redland Court (High School), Bristol (Fig. 150), we see a gate with two unusually wide side panels and a not ungraceful overthrow, which, nevertheless, seems scarcely dignified enough for its somewhat rich setting.

On the other hand, the rough ivy-clad gate-piers at Redland Green Chapel (Fig. 149) seem an uncouth frame for the delicate overthrow which spans the gates, although the latter are made of stronger stuff and have a more simple and primitive aspect. The chapel, seen in the background, is said to have been designed by Strong of Bristol, though a local tradition relates that Sir Christopher Wren had a hand in it.

We cannot do better than bring this chapter to a close with a reference to one of the last pieces of ironwork of this century, about which discussion as to the date of execution is improbable. The cast and wrought iron gates and overthrow to the north door of St. Nicholas' Church (Fig. 228, page 180) are 10ft. 3ins. wide, and their scale, massive appearance and uninteresting detail forebode the fate of ironworking in the next century and the coming of the earlier Gothic revival. On the upper horizontal of the overthrow is cast the name of the firm (not the smith) which executed this work—Harford and Co.—and the place and date, Bristol, 1791. This can be clearly seen in the illustration. The cast-iron railings to the John Whitson monument in the north porch of the same church illustrate a later and more complete abandonment of wrought iron, and the unhealthy copyist movement which accompanied the adoption of factory methods and cheaply made cast iron.

An effective contrast with the above cast-iron railings (illustrations of which occur in the last chapter) is afforded by the essentially graceful, yet undoubtedly sturdy, wrought-iron railings from Albemarle Row, Bristol (Figs. 154 and 155). There is no question as to which is the finer in design, in workmanship or in the texture of the finished iron, and it is doubtful even whether the cast iron has the advantage in point of sheer strength and fitness for its purpose.

Below is given a brief but interesting account of Elmore Court, Gloucestershire, and the great gates, which are attributed to William Edney :

There is an engraving by Kyp in Atkins' *Gloucestershire*. It represents a typical William III house with hipped roof, a nine-windowed front, formal grounds and walled gardens, of which the principal one is entered, opposite the centre of the house, through wrought-iron gates. These are certainly correctly drawn, as they exactly represent those which now form the entrance to Elmore and which were brought from Rendcombe before that place was sold in the

156.—GATES, TREDEGAR PARK, MON.

nineteenth century. . . . The gates . . . have all the appearance of being the work of William Edney . . . much good work . . . is due to him [including Fig. 156], the exceedingly fine example at Tredegar Park in Monmouthshire. [These and the evidence of Edney's handiwork are referred to elsewhere.] . . . His embossed work, principally composed of acanthus foliage, was not equal to that of Tijou or some of his other followers, but was certainly better than we find on the Elmore gates and it must be surmised that this decidedly perishable form of iron ornamentation was found in bad condition when the gates were removed from Rendcombe to Elmore, and was replaced by a far less expert nineteenth century hand. But the design and all the main details bear evidence of being Edney's work, and should be compared with the gates of Tewkesbury Abbey, which he is believed to have executed for Lord Gage in 1734.—(" T." in *Country Life*, Vol. xxxvi, No. 938, page 851.)

157.—GATES, TEWKESBURY ABBEY.

CHAPTER VIII
THE MIDLAND SMITHS

Mr. Bakewell has finisht your work, of the arbor. . . . he has just got a shop fitting up at derby he is so miserable poor that I believe he cant remove till he has some money.

THE tragedy of Robert Bakewell's early struggles is clearly recorded in this poignant paragraph. The quotation is taken from a letter written by Elizabeth Coke to her brother Thomas, and a photograph of this is shown in Fig. 159. There is no date on this interesting letter, but it was probably written in 1708, although the date has been given as April 8th, 1711. It refers to the iron trelliswork " arbor " which Bakewell made at Melbourne, Derbyshire, illustrations of the exterior and interior of which appear below. This

158.—THE " ARBOR," MELBOURNE, DERBYSHIRE, BY ROBERT BAKEWELL. 1706.

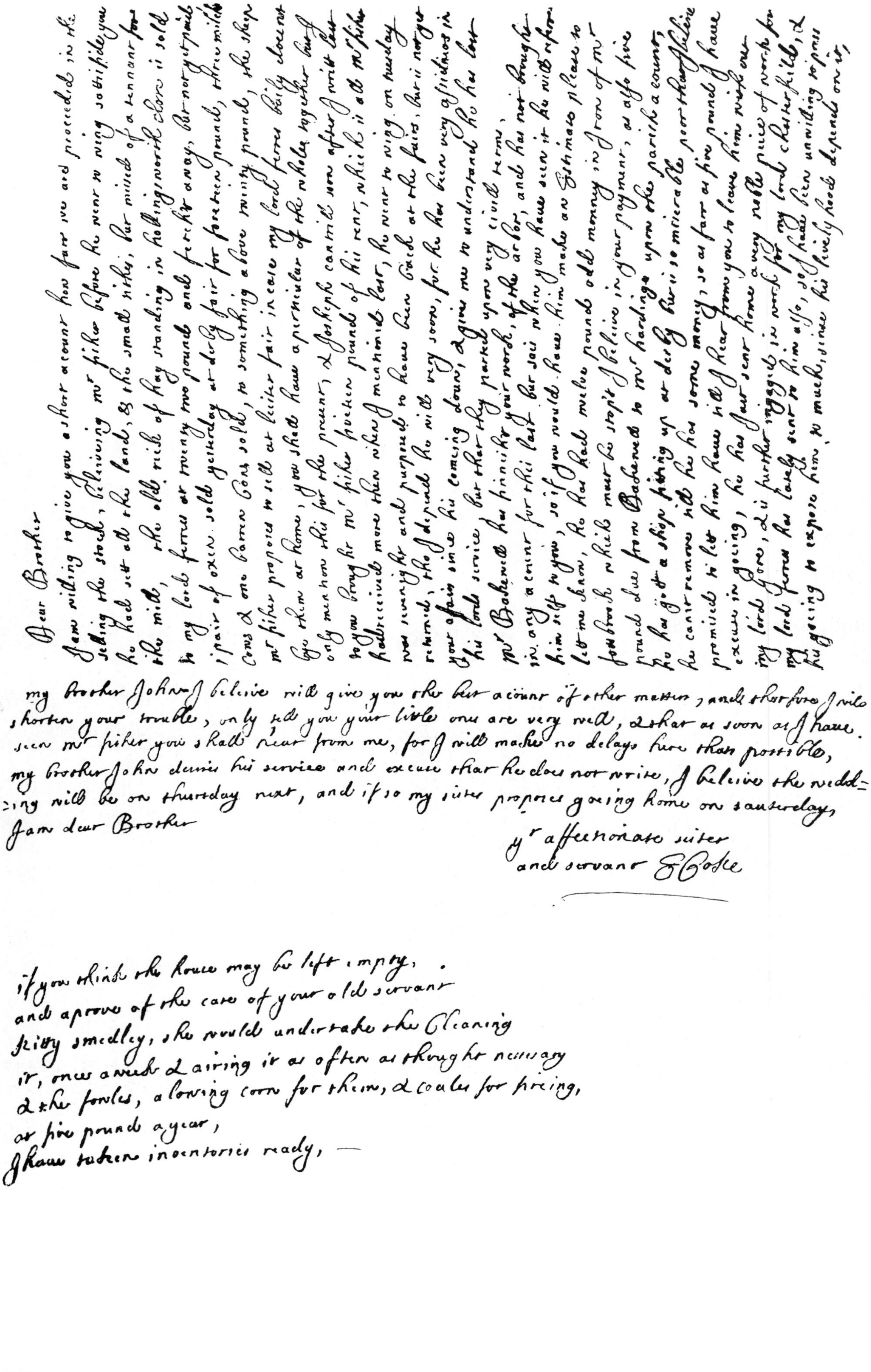

Dear Brother

I am willing to give you a short acount how farr we are proceeded in the selling the stock, believing mr piker before he went to wing sattisfide you he had sett all the land, & the small tithes, but missed of a tennant for the mill, the old rick of hay standing in hollingsworth close is sold to my lord ferrers at twenty two pounds and fetcht away, but not yet paid 1 pair of oxen sold yesterday at derby fair for foreteen pounds, three milch cows & one barren cow sold, to something above twenty pound, the sheep mr piker proposes to sell at leiter fair incase my lord ferrers baily does not bye them at home, you shall have a perticular of the whole together but I only mention this for the present, & Joseph cantrill soon after I writt last to you brought mr piker fiveteen pounds of his rent, which is all mr piker hath received more then when I mentioned last, he went to wing on tuesday was sevenight and purposed to have been back at the fairs, but is not yet returned, tho I depend he will very soon, for he has been very assiduous in your afairs since his comeing down, & gives me to understand he has lost his lords service, but that they parted upon very civill terms,

mr Bakewell has finisht your work, of the arbor, and has not brought in any acount for this last but sais when you have seen it he will reffer him self to you, so if you would have him make an Estimate please to lett me know, he has had twelve pounds odd monny in Iron of mr fossbrook which must be stop't I believe in your payment, as also five pound due from Bakewell to mr hardinge upon the parish acount, he has gott a shop fitting up at derby but is so miserable poor that I believe he cannt remove till he has some money, so as farr as five pound I have promised to lett him have till I hear from you to leave him without excuse in going, he has Just sent home a very noble piece of work for my lord Gore, & is further ingaged in work for my lord chesterfield, & my lord ferrers has lately sent to him also, so I have been unwilling to press his going to expose him so much, since his lively hood depends on it,

my brother John I believe will give you the best acount of other matters, and therfore I will shorten your trouble, only tell you your little ones are very well, & that as soon as I have seen mr piker you shall hear from me, for I will make no delays here than possible, my brother John desires his service and excuse that he does not write, I believe the wedd-ing will be on thursday next, and if so my sister proposes going home on saturday,

I am dear Brother

yr affectionate sister
and servant E Coke

if you think the house may be left empty,
and aprove of the care of your old servant
kitty smedley, she would undertake the Cleaning
it, once a week & airing it as often as thought necessary
& the fowles, alowing corn for them, & coales for fireing,
at five pound a year,
I have taken inventories ready,

159.—FACSIMILE OF LETTER FROM ELIZABETH COKE TO THOMAS COKE, HER BROTHER, DATE 1708 OR 1711.

quaint conceit is full of charming and graceful work when examined in detail. Bakewell was one of the English smiths who drew his inspiration from Tijou, but the former's work, nevertheless, displays great individuality, especially in a lightness of touch and a capacity for design well illustrated in this example.

There is at the present time a very intelligent and well known old local smith who has had many restoration jobs to do on Bakewell's work. This old craftsman has discovered Robert Bakewell's mark, a tracing from a rubbing of which is shown in the illustration which forms the tailpiece to this chapter, and he makes the suggestion that, though the letters now appear slightly raised, they were, in fact, not so originally, but sunk: his idea is that, in stamping them, the blow of the hammer compressed, hardened and, so to say, crystallised the metal, and when the surrounding softer iron corroded, the letters were left standing up. The rubbing of the mark in question was taken from a bar of the gates of the old Derby Silk Mill.

The monogram or cypher surmounting these gates, which is in the circle in the centre of the overthrow, is probably that of Sir *Thomas* Lombe—not of John Lombe, as has usually been recorded in this connection.

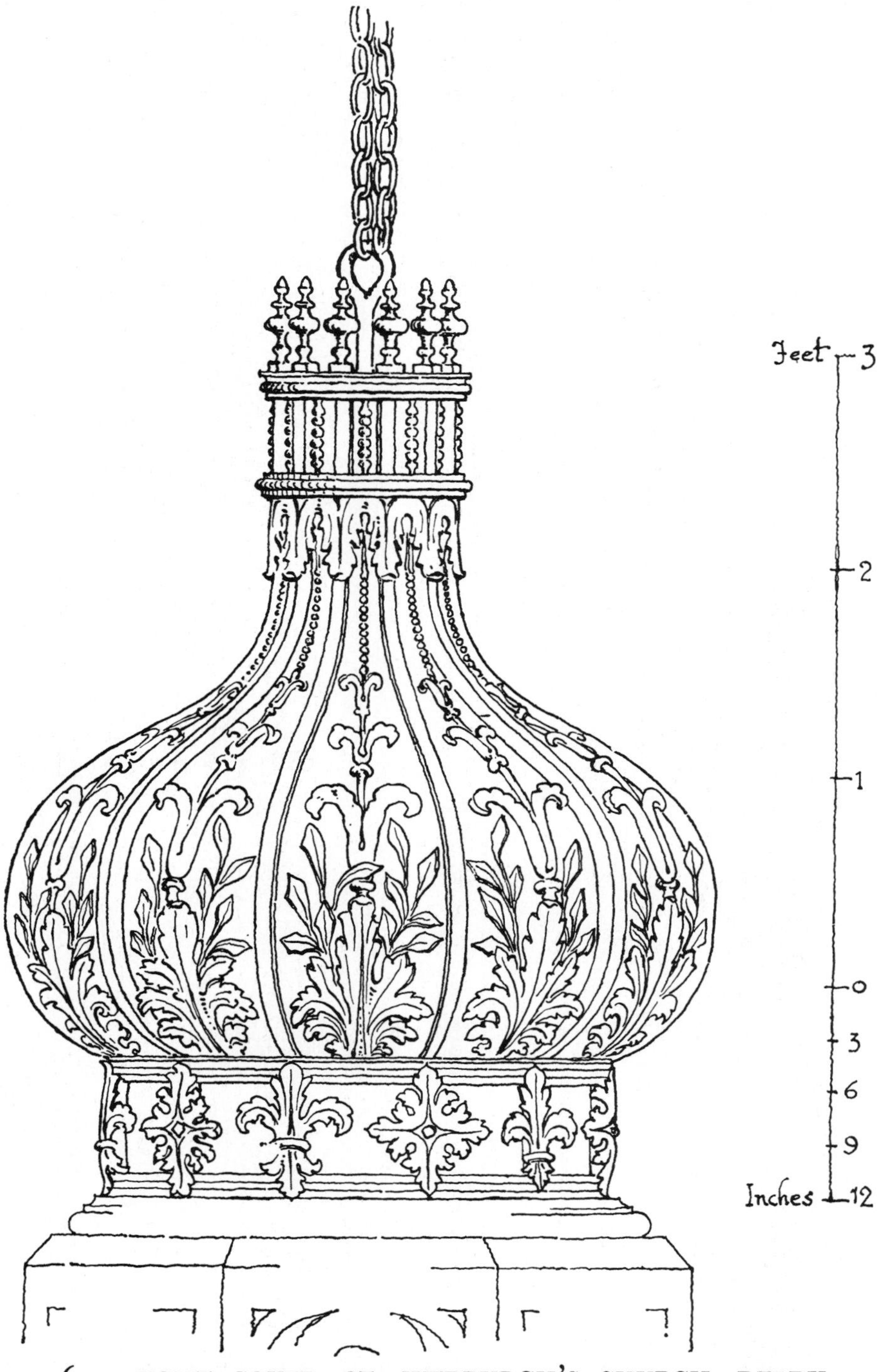

160.—FONT COVER, ST. WERBURGH'S CHURCH, DERBY.
(From a drawing kindly supplied by Mr. G. A. Cope.)

John and Thomas, his brother, together managed the Derby Silk Mill, but John was the technical expert and Thomas the organiser and business manager of the firm (*Dictionary of National Biography*). The old Silk Mill gates were made in 1717. They illustrate how charmingly Bakewell welded grace to strength, and with what apparent ease the English smiths, though

161.—STAUNTON HAROLD CHURCH: THE FIRST EARL'S SCREEN.

162.—THE STAIRCASE, STAUNTON HAROLD, LEICESTERSHIRE.

163.—GATES, PENSHURST, KENT.

benefiting by Tijou's example, soon equalled, and in some cases surpassed, the achievements of the master.

In All Saints' Church, Derby, are preserved many of the works of Bakewell's hand. The gates, altar rail and Cavendish screen, parts of which have been altered and moved since his day, very greatly enhance the effect of James Gibbs' nave and chancel. The parish records, showing the payments made to Bakewell on account of this work, are still extant, and they were published in *Chronicles of the Collegiate Church of All Saints Derby*, by Dr. Charles Cox and Mr. (later Sir) St. John Hope in 1881. On page 81 Dr. Cox writes :

> Several details of the interior will be spoken of in subsequent chapters, but the beautiful screen of wrot iron is too essential a portion of the fabric to be included in any account of the fittings especially when we know that it formed an essential part of Gibbs's design. The screen divided off the East end of the church, at the second pillar from that end from the rest of the building, etc. . . . The screen was the work of a native of Derby, Mr Bakewell, for which he was paid £338. 10/-.

Also, in a footnote on the same page occurs the following :

> The parish also paid him £50 for the western gates in the Churchyard, which were, alas ! removed during the recent alteration and sold by auction.

The following is an extract from the same work :

. . . in 1873–4 the church was entirely reseated, repainted and otherwise "beautified." The alterations included the building of a commodious vestry at the East end of the church and the utilising for seats of the two sides of the chancel. But this plan unfortunately involved the disturbance and loss of much of Bakewell's excellent Ironwork* and rendered ridiculous the elaborate Cavendish monument.

[*Considerable opposition was made to the interference with the ironwork by several of the most influential parishioners. An opposition to the grant of the Faculty was entered in the Consistory Court Lichfield, but eventually a compromise was come to, by which it was agreed that "the side railings and gates of the Devonshire chapel and vestry should be placed on the north and south sides of the 'Communion space' . . ." This agreement has not been carried out. The railings were thus placed but the gates have been sold or otherwise disposed of ; moreover, the old gates of the chancel itself have been illegally removed and now lie with a lot of other débris in the town vault. Other parts of the ironwork are also missing.]

The modern screens to match the old were put in in 1904. They were made by Mr. E. Haslam of Derby under the superintendence of Mr. Temple Moore. The old gates, which, according to Dr. Cox, were found lying in the town vault, were brought out, repaired and re-fixed by the present vicar.

An old inscription in the church reads thus :

The old church was begun to be taken down Feb Ye 18th 1722-3. The first sermon was preached in the New Church Novem^r^ 21st 1725 by Ye Rev^d^ Dr Hutchinson.

164.—GATES AT LONGFORD HALL, DERBYSHIRE.

165.—GATES, PLAS LLANRYDD.

The following are extracts from the parish records :

(*a*) List of subscriptions towards cost of new fabric.
Total £4,162 13. 6d.

(*b*) List of accounts of Expenditure.

(I) To Contractors A.D. 1723.
(II) ,, ,, 1724.
(III) ,, ,, 1725.

including dates to December 10th and followed by list commencing December 14th, including :

To Mr Gibbs for Plan of church	25 : 0 : 0
,, Hulsborgh for Copper plate and 300 plates	12 : 17 : 8
,, Dinner to Commissioners etc.	7 : 17 : 5

And :

To Mr Bakewell	100 : 0 : 0
,, ,, more	10 : 0 : 0
,, ,, ,, ...	30 : 0 : 0
,, ,, ,, ...	21 : 0 : 0

The total disbursed for Bakewell is, therefore, £161. In the churchwardens' accounts for 1730–31, in addition to various other smaller items paid in that and previous years by the parish out of the ordinary expenditure, occurs the following entry :

. . . Contractors etc. including
To Mr. Bakewell for Ironwork in the Church 157. 10. 9

The foregoing £161, with this £157 10s. 9d., makes a total of £318 10s. 9d., which represents the whole cost of the ironwork put in by Bakewell.

Though examination has failed to reveal his mark upon it, a Bakewell's grace, vigour and skill are portrayed in the interesting and unusual font-cover in St. Werburgh's Church, Derby. It is possible, however, that this is the handiwork of one of his apprentices, but, in any case, it does great credit to the Midland smiths. A search in the parish accounts of this time revealed an entry of a payment to Bakewell for a pair of sconces for the chancel (which have since disappeared), but failed to reveal any record of payment to him for the font-cover. The latter has suffered some vicissitudes since Bakewell's day. Some thirty-five years ago the late Bishop Suffragan of Derby, who was also its vicar, built a large new church alongside the old church and tower. The late Sir Arthur Blomfield was the architect for this work, and he ingeniously incorporated the old buildings as a side chapel off the nave of his new church. During the progress of these works the font-cover was discovered, sadly broken and disfigured by rust, in an old cellar. It was forthwith restored and a new font was made for it, and a chain with

166.—GATES, OKEOVER HALL, DERBYSHIRE.

rise and fall balance-weight was made to attach it to the baptistery ceiling, where it still hangs at the present day.

There is a fine wrought-iron screen in Staunton Harold Church, Leicester, which is believed to be the work of Bakewell. In the photograph of the letter which Elizabeth Coke wrote to her brother, Vice-Chamberlain Coke, can be seen the following words :

> . . . he has just sent home a very noble piece of work for my lord Gore [Gower] and is further engaged in work for my lord Chesterfield, and my lord ferrers has lately sent to him also, . . .

The " lord ferrers " probably commissioned Bakewell to make the Staunton screen about this time. Sir Robert Shirley was created Viscount Tamworth and Earl Ferrers by Queen Anne in 1711, and the screen bears his arms

167.—GATE PIER, OKEOVER, DERBYSHIRE.

168.—GATES, OKEOVER, DERBYSHIRE.

and coronet wrought in the overthrow above the gates. This is, both in its proportions and its details, a remarkably fine piece of work.

Longford Hall, Derbyshire, boasts an unusually interesting pair of gates which are attributed to Bakewell.

The Penshurst gates, also by Bakewell, are a typical example of this craftsman's best work. The shape, proportions and lozenge with centre wave bar of the curved overthrow are seen again in Plas Llanrydd and Okeover gates. The gates at Mr. Stanley Weyman's house, Plas Llanrydd, have a striking similarity to those at Penshurst ; so much so that it is quite likely that the latter were also executed by Bakewell. It is, nevertheless, customary to attribute these gates to the Davies brothers, and they may have been worked on by them when they were with Bakewell.

There is a great quantity of fine wrought ironwork at Okeover Hall, Derby. The Okeover demesne was granted between the years 1096 and 1113 by Nigil, Abbot of Burton, to Ormus de Acouvere, and it has been in the possession of the Okeover family to the present day. " The oaks certainly gave name to the place, whose designation signifies an ' over ' against a riverside or valley where oaks grew. Some physical characteristic nearly always gave name to a place, and from the place, as in this instance, the family derived its patronymic " (*Country Life*, Vol. XI, page 176). Mr. Avray Tipping, in *English Homes*, says :

169.—GARDEN GATES, OKEOVER HALL, DERBYSHIRE.

> Okeover, on the Stafford-Derbyshire border, being a very ancient fabric, often altered and contiguous to its church, did not lend itself to a formal and balanced forecourt. But its early eighteenth century owner gave great employment to Bakewell, the Derby smith, who had fully absorbed the technique of Tijou, so that the Okeover gates with their supporting piers are an admirable example of the co-operation of the stonemason and the smith in the adornment of the adjuncts of the house under the late Stuarts.

Referring to the staircase balustrade, both Mr. Starkie Gardner and Mr. Avray Tipping have previously suggested the possibility that this is by Robert Bakewell, owing to its similarity to other work known to be by this smith, and there would appear to be no doubt whatever that they are correct in this assumption, when it is noticed that the balustrade to the stair in Okeover Hall is an exact replica of that at Staunton Harold, where there is actual proof that the ironwork was by Robert Bakewell.

At the Baptist Chapel, St. Mary's Gate, Derby, there is an exceptionally fine side gate bearing many of the marks of Bakewell's genius. This shows the typical openwork shell design referred to in the chapter on the Welsh smiths, which the Davies brothers, no doubt, copied direct from Bakewell, as they are known to have worked with him in the early part of their career, and it is obvious that they adopted features from widely different sources in their cruder and, so to say, prentice work. The ornament filling the arched overthrow is somewhat weak in conception, but, in the main, this side gate is a more pleasing design than the rather dull main gates. The latter are only saved from complete dullness by their sprightly scrolled overthrow.

170.—STAIRCASE BALUSTRADE, OKEOVER HALL, DERBYSHIRE.

In conclusion, we may sum up Robert Bakewell's contribution to English ironwork thus : He undoubtedly added something fine and typically British to the Tijou manner, and helped more than most of his contemporaries to raise the level of craftsmanship and design.

171.—ROBERT BAKEWELL'S MARK.

CHAPTER IX

MISCELLANEOUS EXAMPLES

IN this chapter we shall include many of the beautiful examples of old English ironwork which, either because they are the work of unknown smiths or because their date is uncertain, could not be included in the foregoing chapters.

The first illustration gives a happy example of the value of silhouette in garden ironwork. The house, which is faintly seen in the background, is Crowhurst Place, a residence of the Duchess of Marlborough. It is a moated fifteenth century building, but with extensive modern additions and gardens designed by Mr. Crawley.

172.—GATES, CROWHURST PLACE.

Chesterfield House, Mayfair, a residence of Viscount Lascelles, was completed in 1749 for the fourth Earl of Chesterfield by Isaac Ware. The fine staircase balustrade was not a part of the architect's design, for, " like the marble steps and columns of stair and screens, it came from Canons when that seat was pulled down in 1727. . . . The iron and marble work . . . had nothing to do with Ware except that he was constrained to arrange his plan for their inclusion.

173.—STAIRCASE BALUSTRADE FROM CANONS PARK, NOW AT CHESTERFIELD HOUSE.

They were the spoils of the Duke of Chandos' short-lived mansion of Canons, and hence the columns of the screen are called by Lord Chesterfield ' Canonical pillars.' "[1] Canons (or Canons Park, as it is now known), a palace built by the first Duke of Chandos at Edgware between 1712 and 1720, was designed on an absurdly extravagant scale. Edward Strong the younger, who did the final work to St. Paul's Cathedral, is said to have been the builder. The architects are believed to have been James of Greenwich, Gibbs and Shepherd, while John

[1] *Country Life*, Vol. LI, page 238.

174.—GATES TO LILY POOL TERRACE, BODNANT, DENBIGHSHIRE.

Price probably did the drawings only. In 1747 the house was sold in separate lots. Mr. Starkie Gardner states that the staircase and some railings went to Chesterfield House, and the iron gates to The Durdans, Hampstead Parish Church, and, possibly, to Wotton. He says: "The Durdans possesses richly worked iron gates still bearing the Chandos motto. . . . The not dissimilar gates of the Hampstead Parish Church bear no arms, but their purchase from Canons with about 59 feet of railings is recorded in the Minute Book of the Church Trustees. . . ."

175.—GATES, FROM THE WILD GARDEN, COMPTON BEAUCHAMP, SHRIVENHAM, BERKS.

By whom the staircase balustrade and the other magnificent ironwork was made is a disputed point. The design was probably by Tijou, but the execution of the work must have been handed over to one of his most expert pupils, for, while the workmanship is that of the master, yet he left England in 1712, the year in which the house was begun.

A pair of charming little gates in the garden at Bodnant, Denbighshire, a seat of Lord and Lady Aberconway, is illustrated in Fig. 174. They fill the arched gateway into the lily pond terrace, one of the beautiful hanging terraces which form a feature of this garden. "The central recess has a tablet bearing the inscription, 'These Terrace Gardens were designed by Henry

176.—NEAR VIEW OF THE SCREEN, COMPTON BEAUCHAMP (BELOW).

177.—SCREEN AND GATES, FROM FORECOURT, COMPTON BEAUCHAMP.

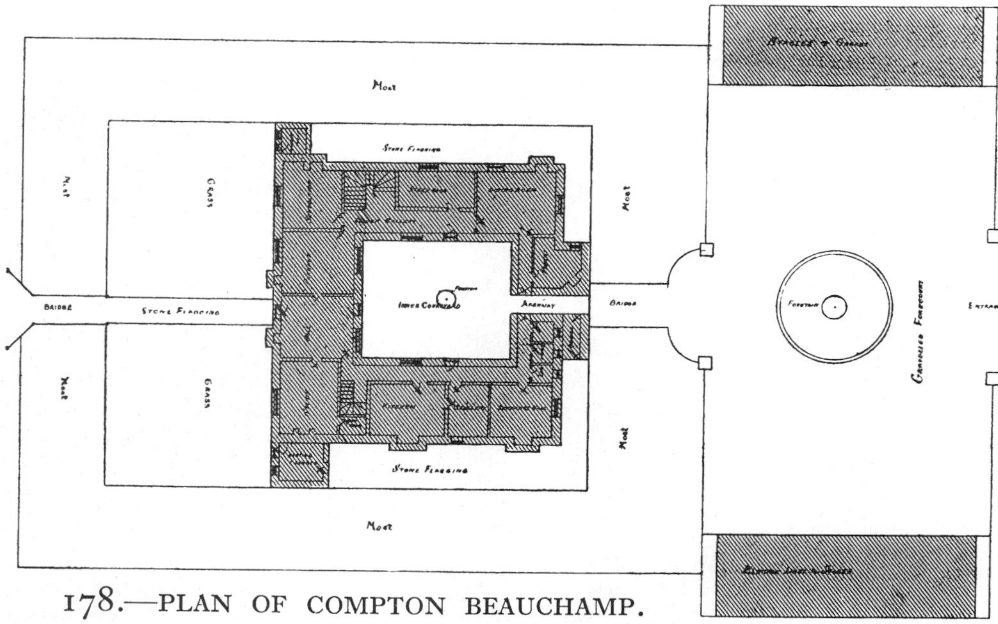

178.—PLAN OF COMPTON BEAUCHAMP.

179.—THE GATES, FROM THE WIG AVENUE, COMPTON BEAUCHAMP.

Duncan McLaren 1905.' "[2] There is no other clue to the history of the gates, but in the design of the flower, where silhouette is abandoned for outline treatment in flat iron, they resemble the gates in the Wrexham Church altar rail, where the tendrils between scrolls are carried out in this manner. (These are illustrated in the chapter on "Wales.")

The delicate garden gates at Emral, near Wrexham, do not show this particular treatment, but might well be by the same smith; and here, again, the scrolls are bound together by moulded

180.—GARDEN GATE, NORTON CONYERS, MELMERBY, YORKS.

181.—SIDE GATE TO DEER PARK, BELTON HOUSE, LINCS.

collars. The fact that these three examples are in the same locality lends colour to the idea that they may all have come from the same anvil.

The illustration (Fig. 175) of the gates of the wild garden to Compton Beauchamp, near Shrivenham, Berkshire, shows the overthrow which encloses a rectangular panel containing the monogram "A.R.," with a second "R" reversed, probably for symmetry. These letters might be the initials of the Miss Anne Richards who was the owner

[2] *Country Life*, Vol. XLVIII, page 84.

182.—GATES TO THE WEST FORECOURT, BELTON HOUSE, LINCOLNSHIRE.

of Compton Beauchamp at the close of the eighteenth century. The house is of Tudor date, with Palladian additions, made, possibly, at the time of Miss Richards' occupancy. Another pair of gates (Figs. 176 - 179) closes the "Wig Avenue" and opens on the forecourt. These gates are very unusual (especially in the double whorl given to the feet of the dog-bars), and their setting gives them an added dignity. The Wig Avenue gets its name from a custom of the eighteenth century, when the local gentry, dismounting here, put on their wigs before advancing to the house to call on Miss Richards![3] The old plan (Fig. 178) shows the original moated house approached by bridges, and the forecourt and gates which were probably added when the Palladian front was built.

183.—GATES AND RAILINGS TO QUEEN'S HOUSE (ONCE KNOWN AS TUDOR HOUSE), CHELSEA.

Of the illustrations following, Fig. 181 shows the side gate to the deer park at Belton House, Lincolnshire. The house was designed by Wren, being begun in 1685 and finished in 1688, while further additions were made during a period of about forty years. There seems to be no record of the name of the smith, but the design is reminiscent of the work of Thomas Robinson, who worked under Wren at St. Paul's Cathedral. The gates and piers remain in their original position at the entrance from the Grantham Road to the great avenue that stretches up to the house. Lord Tyrconnel quartered other arms with those of Brownlow, and adopted lion supporters in place of his ancestors' greyhounds. It is these quartered arms that appear on the overthrow of his gates, while the lions surmount his gate-piers.[4]

[3] *Country Life*, Vol. VI, page 787. [4] *Country Life*, Vol. XXX, page 315.

184.—WEST ENTRANCE GATES, ARBURY HALL, WARWICKSHIRE.

The larger illustration shows the smaller gates to the west court. ". . . Sir John Brownlow, who was created Viscount Tyrconnel in 1718, and died in 1754, made many changes at Belton House. It was he who began the fine library and laid out the beautiful formal gardens, which no longer remain. Perhaps to his time we may ascribe these noble hammered gates of the west forecourt, and other external adornments."[5] Mr. Starkie Gardner states that of three forecourt screens two belong to the house, while the third was brought from Hough in 1743 (*loc. cit.*, page 90). The house is famous for its wood carvings by Grinling Gibbons.

The little gate to the garden at Norton Conyers, Melmerby, Yorks, of which an illustration is given, is a very pleasing example. The knocker, hung on the central standard, is a quaint feature of this design, which, whatever its date, is full of charm (it is attributed to Warren by Mr. Starkie Gardner, page 103). Norton Conyers is the magnificent seat of the

185.—ENTRANCE GATES AND SIDE WICKETS, BURLEY-ON-THE-HILL, RUTLAND.

Grahams, which stands on the banks of the Ure. The family crest—a pair of wings addorsed—can be seen surmounting the overthrow.

The gate to Queen's House (once known as Tudor House), No. 16, Cheyne Walk, Chelsea, ". . . has all the characteristics of the best period of Late Renaissance Ironwork in England." Rossetti once lived here, and the name of the house is said to owe its origin to the story that Catherine of Braganza lived here also. The story is, however, generally regarded as a legend. The oval panel in the overthrow bears a monogram made up of the letters " R " and " C," both of which are reversed.

A pair of gates at the west entrance to Arbury Hall, Warwickshire, has an interesting overthrow of early form. The centre panel bears the shield of Newdigate and Twisden, and

[5] *Country Life*, Vol. XIV, page 619.

the whole is surmounted by a fleur-de-lis, which is either a survival from a previous epoch or a subsequent clumsy addition. No mention of the smith is made, but it is recorded that Wren designed the stables, and probably, therefore, one of his London smiths made the gates (Starkie Gardner, *op. cit.*, page 230, says: " There are railings at Arbury Hall which may be Robinson's work "). He attributes these gates, however, to Warren, though he says they " correspond in some details with Edney's work " (*loc. cit.*, page 192). It is recorded on page 95 of Grinling Gibbons' book that one, Robert Edney, witnesses the agreement between Newdigate of Arbury and Grinling Gibbons, in 1693. Who more likely to be at hand as a witness than the smith? Yet Edney, the smith, was William, so that Robert may have been a son, a follower of his father's craft and possibly the maker of the Arbury ironwork.

186.—STAIRCASE BALUSTRADE IN STABLE BUILDINGS, BURLEY-ON-THE-HILL.

At Burley-on-the-Hill, Rutland, is an exceptionally fine set of entrance gates and side wicket gates, the cresting to which carries through the main outline of the central overthrow. They were executed in 1700–4 by Joshua Lord, probably from designs by Tijou. " They have the flower work and yet the restraint which the English followers of Tijou did not always achieve, and are, moreover, contained by two fine fluted pillars." Joshua Lord is only a name, but his work shows that he deserves to be honoured as a master of his craft. An old drawing provides evidence that the iron gates were an afterthought, wooden ones having been originally intended. Formerly two little lodges flanked the gates.[6]

The balustrading to the western garden entrance is less successful both in scale and in design, and that to the south door is poor. On the other hand, the simple balustrades in the stable buildings are as unaffectedly charming as they could well be.

[6] *Country Life*, Vol. XLIII, page 178.

187.—STAIRCASE BALUSTRADE IN STABLE BUILDINGS, BURLEY-ON-THE-HILL.

In contemplating these designs one realises that perfect design and workmanship are not dependent on period, for these railings might as well be the product of a master of the modern school as of the year 1700.

Kimbolton Castle, the seat of the Duke of Manchester, was altered in 1707 by Vanbrugh for the first Earl of Manchester. "The . . . illustration gives a presentment of the fine wrought-iron gates that open from the grounds on to the St. Neot's Road. . . . The gates . . . are in the early eighteenth century manner, but the medallions and swags which ornament the frieze of the piers remind one that Robert Adam was employed to design additions to Kimbolton by the fourth Duke." [7]

Fig. 194 illustrates the gates to the President's garden at Magdalen College, Oxford. No details as to date or smith are known, but the design recalls that of the gates to the forecourt at Compton Beauchamp, illustrated on pages 145 and 146. It will be observed that the large husks and clumsy foliage of the overthrow occur also in the latter example. Here, also, the urns surmounting the pilasters exhibit in this design the unusual change from a silhouette to an openwork and line effect.

A vigorous and very unusual design is to be seen in a gate at Packwood, the date of which is said to be about 1700. This is a very good instance of the deplorable effect produced by painting wrought ironwork in white or a light colour, for the unfavourable impression which this illustration gives is largely due to the light colour employed, the halation from which blurs the refinement of the various members.

Petworth House, Sussex, was built in 1686–87, but the handsome gates and railings to the forecourt are, evidently, a later addition (Fig. 191). Whether they were added in the early part of the eighteenth century or were made at a later date is not known.

At Wotton are railings as well as gates, typical of the fine work which is found all over England, but of which little or nothing is known. The illustrations show the house in the background—Wotton House, Aylesbury (the seat of Earl Temple of Stowe)—which was begun

[7] *Country Life*, Vol. xxx, page 474.

188.—WESTERN GARDEN ENTRANCE, BURLEY-ON-THE-HILL.

189.—SOUTH GARDEN ENTRANCE, BURLEY-ON-THE-HILL.

190.—ENTRANCE GATES, ALDERMASTON HALL, BERKS.

in 1704 and completed in 1714. The enclosure of the forecourt by the magnificent iron grille, with a bold curve towards the wings, and the fine panelled urn-crowned gateposts, is a dignified and imposing scheme. The design is reminiscent of Vanbrugh's gates at Eaton Hall. Another delightful example of hammered iron is the gate to the kitchen garden, shown in Fig. 197.

191.—GATES AND SCREEN, PETWORTH HOUSE.

192.—ENTRANCE GATES, KIMBOLTON HOUSE.

193.—GATES, BARLBOROUGH, CHESTERFIELD.

This is an unusually pleasing instance of the happy marriage of iron to brickwork.

Barlborough, Chesterfield, the seat of Miss de Rodes, was completed about 1584 and was built by Francis Rodes, Queen's Serjeant. Mr. Starkie Gardner ascribes the gates to Warren, but later says that they "are perhaps by a London smith" (*loc. cit.*, pages 104 and 198).

194.—GATES TO PRESIDENT'S GARDEN, MAGDALEN COLLEGE, OXFORD.

At Aldermaston Hall, Berkshire, stands a pair of gates also attributed to Warren by Mr. Starkie Gardner. The original manor house was pulled down in 1636 and re-built by Sir Humphrey Forster. It was destroyed by fire in 1848. The gates were erected by Sir W. Coupere, who lived there until the time of the fire. They were made for Lord Stowel of Midgeham House, Berkshire, whose coronet was replaced by the falcon crest of Coupere.

The iron staircase balustrade at Milton, Northamptonshire, is of the same pattern as that at the Great Hall at Holkham, illustrated elsewhere. The date is about 1747, and at this time, probably, the ballroom was built. The gate dates from 1720. It is surmounted with the arms

195.—CAROLEAN TERRACE, PACKWOOD.

of Earl Fitzwilliam (created in 1716), and the shield has "wild men" supporters. Mr. Starkie Gardner remarks that "It recalls the work of Warren" (*loc. cit.*, page 195). There is a smaller gate at Milton, which is another charming example of iron wedded to brickwork.

Inwood House, Somerset, stands on the road from Blandford to Wincanton, close to the village of Hentsbridge. Speaking of the Devonshire House gates under his chapter on Warren, Mr. Starkie Gardner says (*loc. cit.*, pages 102, 148, 150, 152), "They resemble Bakewell's gates at Okeover Hall between piers which are identical with the gate piers at Devonshire House. A lofty wicket gate of precisely the same make and sketched by Ebbets when at Stoke Newington is now at Inwood, near Templecombe." He also speaks of "a small but beautifully designed gate at Inwood near Templecombe," and describes it as having a "boldly scrolled central panel." In describing several Essex gates at Forest Lane, Stratford; Sydenham House, Devon; 15, Cheyne Walk; Easton; a gate at Rainham, etc., he also says, "there is a good gate at Inwood, Templecombe, which must have been produced in the same works."

Kirkleatham Hospital and Hall are situated about two miles from Redcar, Yorkshire. Founded in 1676, the

196.—CAROLEAN TERRACE GATES, PACKWOOD.

197.—GARDEN GATE, WOTTON HOUSE.

buildings were so altered and added to in 1742 that they really belong to that date. They were built by Sir William Turner, Lord Mayor of London, shortly after the Great Fire, and were entirely remodelled by his great-nephew, Cholmley Turner, seventy years later. There is an oblong court with a chapel in the centre of the south end, and in front a semi-circular forecourt with chains and posts. The charity provided for the maintenance of ten poor men and as many poor women, ten boys and ten girls. In remarking upon the excellent ironwork at the Cathedral at York, Mr. Starkie Gardner expresses the hope that other work by the same smith may be found in the country, and goes on to say: "the beautiful gates at Kirklees near Dewsbury

198.—MAIN GATES, WOTTON HOUSE, AYLESBURY.

199.—MAIN GATES, WOTTON HOUSE, AYLESBURY.

200.—GATES AND RAILINGS, KIRKLEATHAM HOSPITAL, REDCAR.

201.—GATES, INWOOD HOUSE, SOMERSET.

202.—GATE, MILTON, NORTHAMPTONSHIRE.

203.—GATES, CARSHALTON PARK, SURREY.

204.—GATES, BEDDINGTON, SURREY.

however . . . forcibly recall those at Devonshire House and Clandon Park. The imposing screen at Kirkleatham near Redcar is of the same work. . . . Probably all are by Warren" (*loc. cit.*, page 206).

Little is known of this smith and his work, and the majority of the examples attributed to him remain as ascribed without further evidence in support or in contradiction.

The gates and screen at Kirkleatham show signs of neglect—or, possibly, not neglect, but, rather, the unwelcome attentions of the "ten poor boys," aided and abetted by the ten girls, which may account for the disappearance of certain leaves and scrolls here and there!

The work shows something in common with that of Robert Bakewell, particularly in the design of the segmental overthrow; but the resemblance is not sufficiently marked to justify any attempt to advance the claims of Bakewell and throw doubt on the claims made for Warren.

Near Croydon there stands the Royal Female Orphan Asylum, which was once known as Beddington Hall. It was built by Sir Francis Carew, the son of Sir Nicholas Carew, who held high office under Henry VIII, but who was eventually beheaded on Tower Hill.

205.—GARDEN GATE, MILTON, NORTHAMPTONSHIRE.

There were two pairs of gates, one pair at the front and one pair at the back of the building, both of which were, unfortunately, sold to an American purchaser in 1913. They thus shared the fate of gates of the same period which, a little earlier, disappeared from the neighbouring

206.—GALLERY LANDING, KIRKLEATHAM.

207.—GATES AT GRIMSTHORPE.

208.—GATES AT KIRKLEATHAM HOSPITAL.

209.—GATE AND PALISADE, HARROWDEN.

210.—STAIRCASE LANDING, GRIMSTHORPE.

211.—THE MAIN GATES, HARROWDEN HALL, NORTHAMPTONSHIRE.

212.—GATES AND PALISADE, NEW COLLEGE, OXFORD.

213.—GATES, TRINITY COLLEGE, OXFORD.

Carshalton Park. That all the gates were probably very fine specimens can be seen from the illustration of the one pair given. Upon the overthrow of these was a panel supported by acanthus scrolls enclosing the monogram "N.C." From the other pair some of the ironwork above the gates was missing, and this is thought to have been the crest and monogram of the ill-fated Sir Nicholas. The ironwork has been attributed to Robinson.

214.—ENTRANCE GATES, LITTLECOTE.

An unfortunate history attaches to the ironwork at Carshalton Park, Surrey. Owned by Sir William Scawen of London, merchant, at his death in 1722 his nephew, who succeeded him employed Levin as architect to prepare designs for a mansion of which the gates and screen formed a part. The house was never built. The total length of the screen is 113ft. The gates are 12ft. wide and 13ft. high. The railings are flanked by stone piers 17ft. high, with lead groups illustrating Actæon and Artemis. As previously mentioned, the gates have been sold. They recall the work of Robinson, and "appear to be by the same hand as the bastion railings at Hampton Court." The pyramidal tops of the gates resemble the screens in St. Paul's. Careful examination of the details renders it almost certain that they are also the work of Thomas Robinson.

Harrowden Hall, Northamptonshire, is the seat of Lord Vaux of Harrowden, who recently restored the fabric. The year when the house

216.—QUENBY COURT GATES.

215.—GARDEN GATE, BALLS PARK, HERTS.

was built is indicated by the rain-water heads, which bear the date 1719. Here are three groups of forecourt gates and screens, all delicate and graceful work in the manner of Thomas Robinson, although they lack the rich acanthus foliage in which he often delighted.

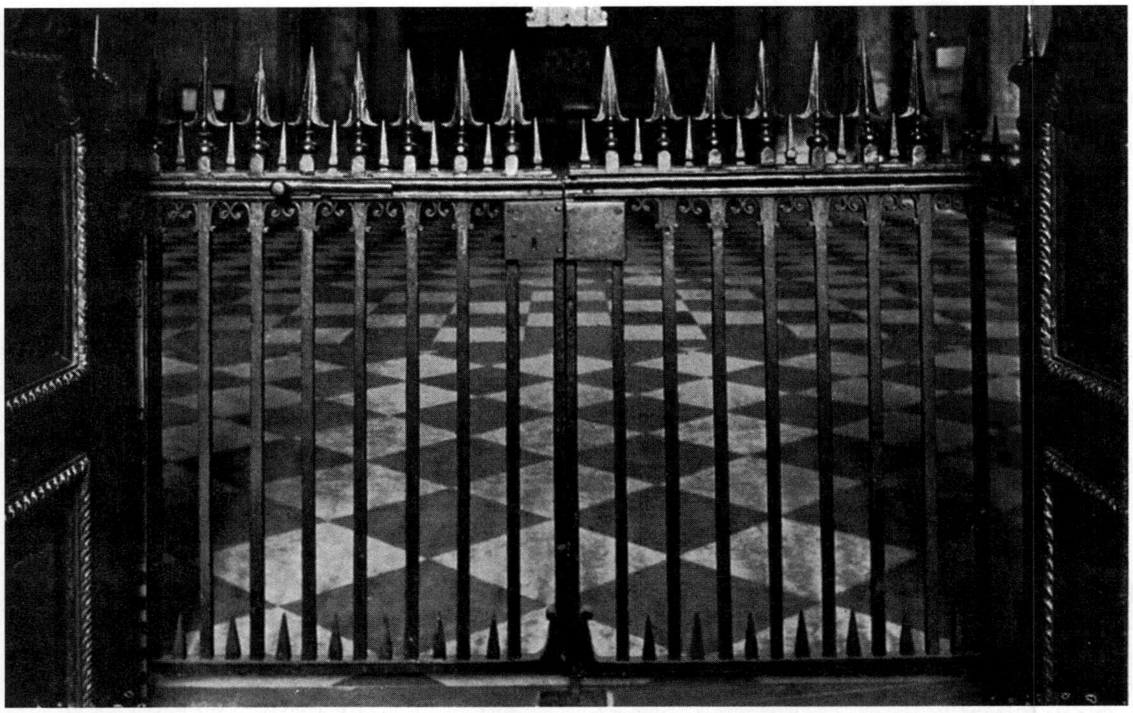

217.—GATES TO CHAPEL OF SS. MICHAEL AND GEORGE, ST. PAUL'S CATHEDRAL.

Grimsthorpe Castle in Lincolnshire is the seat of the Earl of Ancaster. The most recent portion of the buildings was designed by Sir John Vanbrugh in 1720. Of the ironwork, the screen at the entrance has something in common with the work at Belton, and the whole seems reminiscent of Robinson's style, though the name of the smith is uncertain.

The gates at Trinity College, Oxford, were given, in 1737, by a member of the Guildford family. Mr. Starkie Gardner speaks of gates in the garden ; he attributes these to Robinson, their date 1713, and says the gates opening on Broad Street are " simpler and heavier and almost entirely new with the possible exception of parts of the overthrow and the pilaster panels." The illustration appears to be of these gates.

The gates at New College, Oxford, were erected in 1711, and there is a tradition still that they came from the Duke of Chandos' mansion at Canons. Mr. Starkie Gardner ascribes them to Robinson. They are represented in Williams' *Oxford*, 1723–33 ; and Walford, in *Greater London*, definitely states that they came from Canons.

Littlecote, Wiltshire, boasts the finest ironwork in the neighbourhood. It is far too sophisticated to be of local origin, but, unfortunately, it is impossible to say from whose forge it came.

The single gate at Balls Park, Hertford, the seat of Sir Lionel L. Faudel-Phillips, Bt., probably dates from 1720. The panel in the overthrow bears the initials of Edward Harrison, who " augmented and improved " the house at that date. Nothing is known of the smith.

At the church of All Hallows, Barking, stand three of the finest sword or mace stands in London. That on the left has the shield of Sir John Eyles, Lord Mayor in 1726, and the shield of his company, the Haberdashers ; that in the centre bears the shields of Slingsby Bethell,

Lord Mayor in 1755, and of the Fishmongers' Company ; while that on the right has the arms of Sir Thomas Chitty, Lord Mayor in 1759, and of the Salters' Company. Each bears the shield of the City and the Royal arms. The names of the craftsmen who executed these noble designs are unknown.

The fine gates with the quaint figures in the overthrow at Ragley Hall in Alcester, Warwickshire, are all that remain of a remarkable series of gates which once adorned this seat. They date from the first half of the eighteenth century, but nothing is known of their origin.

In the last year of James II and the first of William III Quenby Hall, Leicester, was altered by George Ashby, sheriff of the county ; and the gates (which have been ascribed to Robert Bakewell and to William Edney) were given later by him to Leicester when he re-modelled the approach to the house. They now stand opposite the Art Museum.

218.—BULWICK HALL.

One of the many examples of attribution without sufficient evidence is found at Bulwick Hall, Northamptonshire. The

219.—PAIR OF MACE STANDS FROM PARISH CHURCH, NEWCASTLE-UNDER-LYME, END OF SEVENTEENTH CENTURY.

220.—SUSPENSION ROD FOR CHANDELIER, LATE SEVENTEENTH CENTURY. (*Victoria and Albert Museum.*)

gates have been ascribed to William Edney, but there not only seems to be little internal evidence to justify this, but also the county of Northampton is a long way from Edney's district, and, though this is not a very strong argument, the gates, we think, were probably by a local smith. The date on the entrance colonnade of the house is 1672. The entrance, however, bears the date 1676.

A little known but exceedingly fine staircase exists still in a very good state of preservation

221.—SWORD RESTS, ALL HALLOWS BARKING.

222.—GATES, RAGLEY, WARWICKSHIRE.

at No. 8, Clifford Street, Bond Street, W. The illustrations show that the ironwork of the balustrade was obviously wrought by one of the many excellent smiths of the mid-eighteenth century, but there is no record of the exact date or of the craftsman's name.

In conclusion, it must be noted that the above group of miscellaneous examples does not pretend to be an exhaustive catalogue of the ironwork by unknown smiths. It is merely a representative collection, and most of the examples given are fairly well known and accessible.

223 and 224.—STAIRCASE BALUSTRADE, NO. 8, CLIFFORD STREET, W.

CHAPTER X

THE DECAY AND REVIVAL OF SMITH-CRAFT

WITH the growth of Classic design in England came the natural striving for greater perfection in finish and detail and the elimination of the haphazard work which is, perhaps, the greatest charm of the architecture of the seventeenth and early eighteenth centuries. The culmination in mechanical accuracy was reached in the early nineteenth century, when handwork in every branch of building attained a mathematical exactness and perfection hitherto unequalled. But this accuracy was accompanied by a proportionate loss in that subtle feeling for material, which embraced a sense for texture, colour, and fitness for purpose; the same treatment in design was applied to materials having widely differing qualities. An Adam chimneypiece rich in ornament might equally well be reproduced in marble, wood, iron or plaster. There can be no doubt that this was the result of a gradual growth and improvement in tools, machinery and the earlier forms of mechanical reproduction, such as casting in iron.

225.—WROUGHT-IRON BALUSTERS WITH LEAD AND BRASS ORNAMENT.
Showing Adam influence similar to the more common cast-iron balusters of the time. Late eighteenth century. (Victoria and Albert Museum.)

It is interesting to note how Sir Christopher Wren leapt at the chance of this new form of iron-work, and it is highly characteristic of the man that he saw at once the possibilities which it opened up. The great cast-iron palisade round St. Paul's Cathedral was the earliest attempt at anything of the sort in this country, and its history is indeed

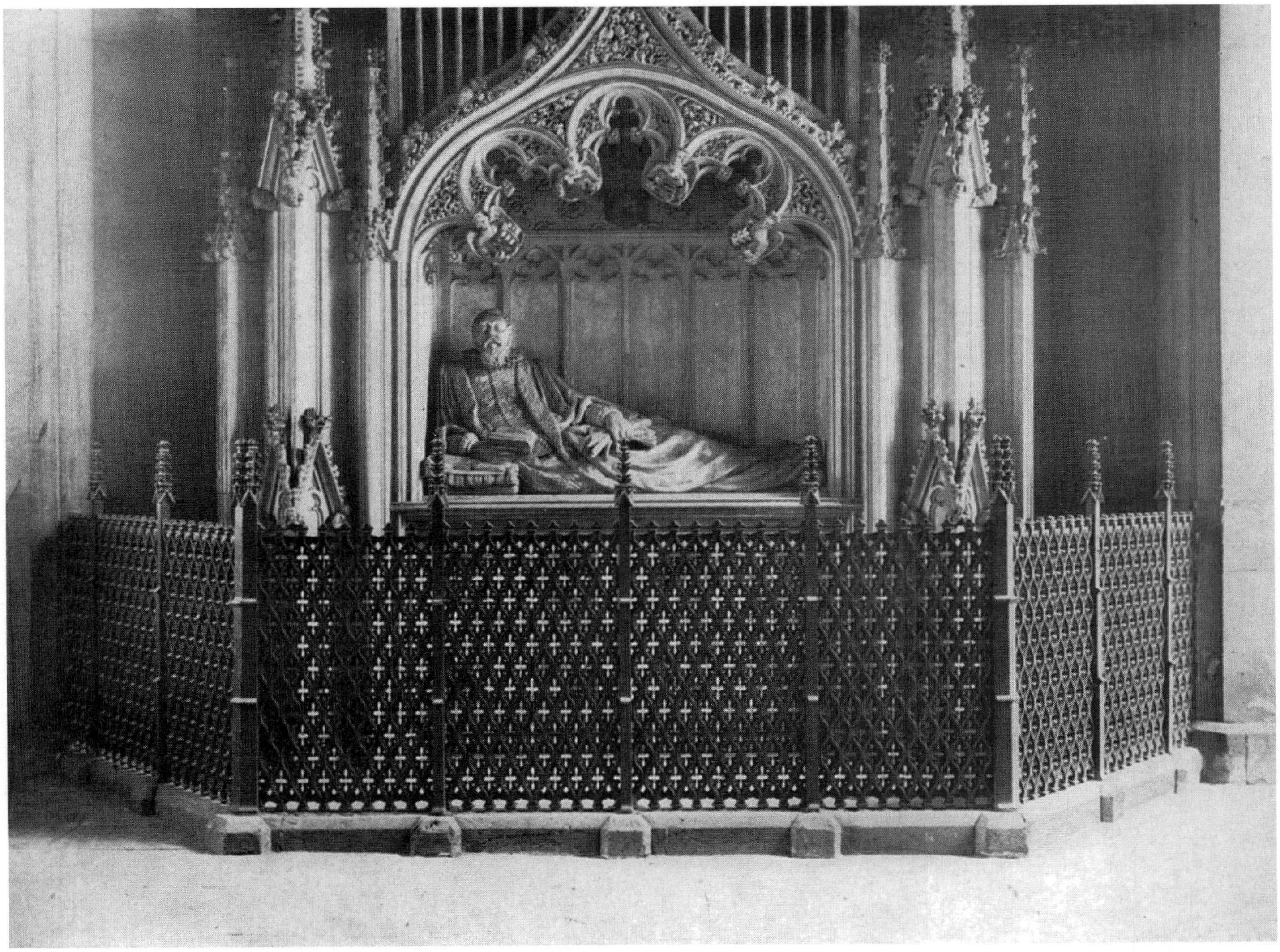

226.—RAIL ROUND THE JOHN WHITSON MONUMENT, ST. NICHOLAS' CHURCH, BRISTOL.

extraordinary. The ultimate cost of these railings reached the staggering total of £11,202 0s. 6d., which, as has already been shown, may be taken to be equal at the present time to between eighty and ninety thousand pounds. Furthermore, the value of cast iron in those days was somewhere in the neighbourhood of 6d. per pound, or approximately 4s. per pound at present values. It is not surprising, therefore, that Sir Christopher had some little difficulty in smoothing out troubles with his clients over this matter.

From then onwards, until the end of the Regency period, an increasing efficiency in this special craft is apparent. English cast iron of that time was unrivalled, and its predecessor, wrought iron, eventually suffered a total eclipse. There is, probably, no trade which shows so clearly the desire of the designer of the period to meet in a proper spirit the trend of the times—that is, to take full advantage of the mechanical devices which were placed before him.

At the same time, however, we see the ever-present desire for the picturesque in the rustic bridges, faked ruins, and so forth, designed and erected by the Adam brothers and their contemporaries, and later the Strawberry Hill—or, as Mr. Clough Williams-Ellis has so happily

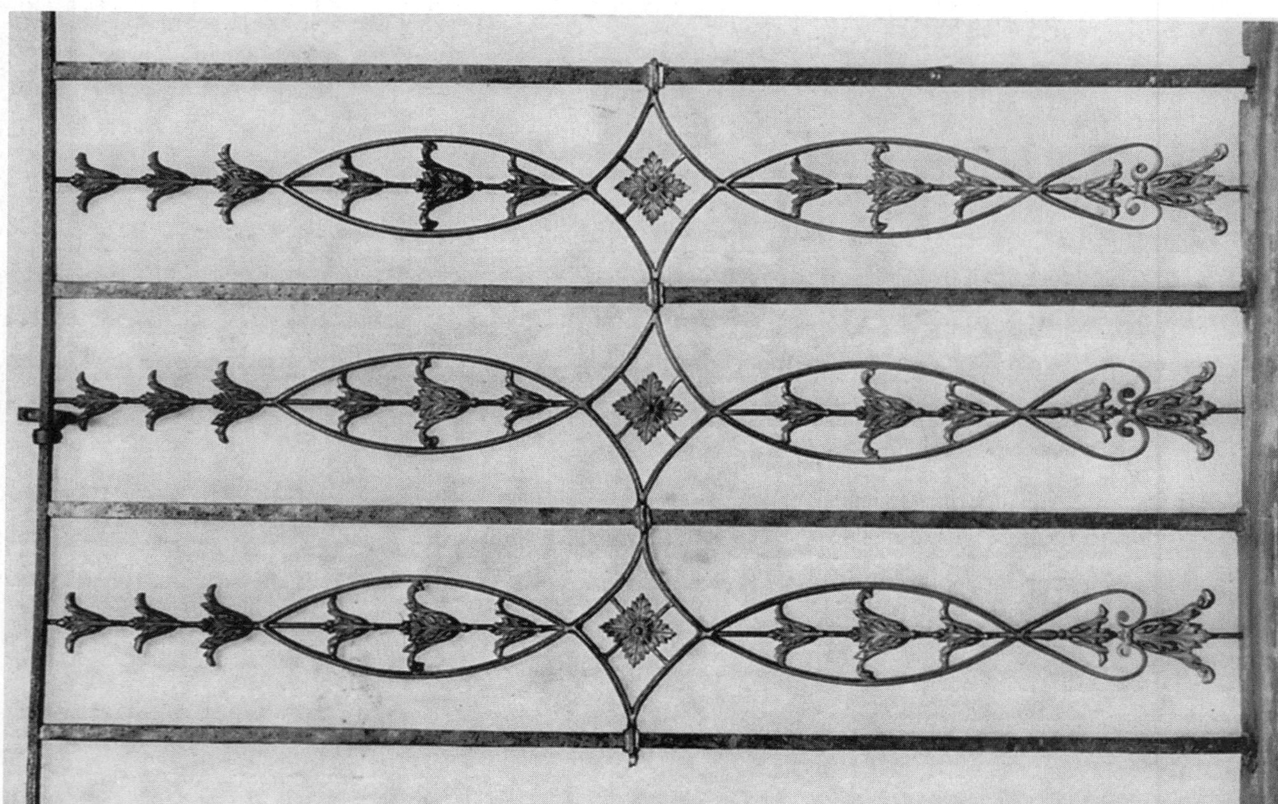

227.—WROUGHT-IRON BALUSTRADE FROM NO. 3, BERNERS STREET, LONDON, 1763.

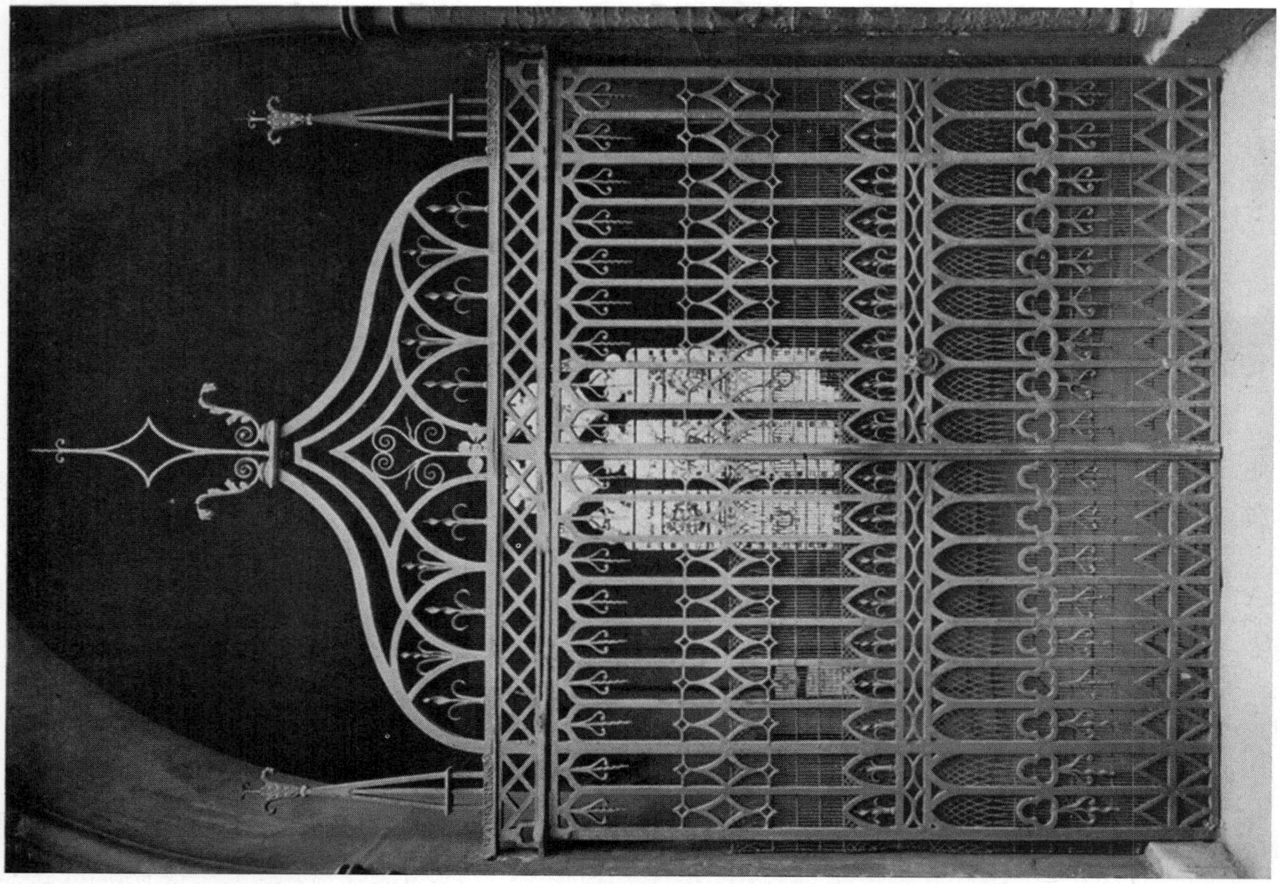

228.—GATES OF NORTH PORCH, ST. NICHOLAS' CHURCH, BRISTOL.

229.—FANLIGHT IN WROUGHT IRON, WITH CAST-LEAD ORNAMENT. (*Victoria and Albert Museum.*)

230.—THE STAIRCASE IN THE ENTRANCE HALL, ASHRIDGE PARK.

named it, the Gentleman's Gothic—manner, which covered the countryside with strange and almost priggish architecture.

With the Victorian era and its shocked abhorrence of everything with a flavour of the degenerate Regency came the Oxford movement, which appears, at first thought, to have been the result of the strenuous exertions of a select but strong few, but which was really, of course, the revulsion of the whole people against a period which, delightful though it was artistically, can have had but little real happiness or comfort for the majority. A man who has triumphantly weathered a great storm or life-threatening crisis receives, when the bitter experience is ended and danger is over, a fresh accession of energy and aspiration, which finds an outlet in a joyous attack upon life's problems, increasing activity and an added power in achievement. A parallel phenomenon is often observed in the life of a nation. The wonderful outburst of energy after the Great Fire of London, accompanied, as it was, by the outpouring of thankfulness of the whole population, resulted in the great movement forward in which the arts were guided by Sir Christopher Wren.

231.—GARDEN GATE IN WROUGHT IRON WITH CAST-LEAD ORNAMENT.
(*The property of Lady Prince Smith.*)

Again, in the nineteenth century, we find the leaders of the Oxford Movement guiding a great popular uprising, a movement spiritual in its inspiration, as all great causes are, yet finding material expression in the endeavour to create beauty in its surroundings. To this movement we owe the revival of taste and individuality, the improvement in craftsmanship and in design which characterise the period.

And now a curious thing happened, for, while the giants of the day who initiated the "Gothic Revival" undoubtedly knew and appreciated to the full the beauties of design and workmanship they were striving to revive, they were unable even to execute drawings which gave anything but a dead cast-iron version of what they wanted. But what was much more serious than ability to draw what they wanted was the fact that there no longer existed the workmen to carry out the work. A century or more of getting down to mechanical accuracy in all materials had produced smiths and craftsmen in all other trades to whom it was, naturally and properly, an effort to produce intentionally the mistakes and blemishes which had given the earlier

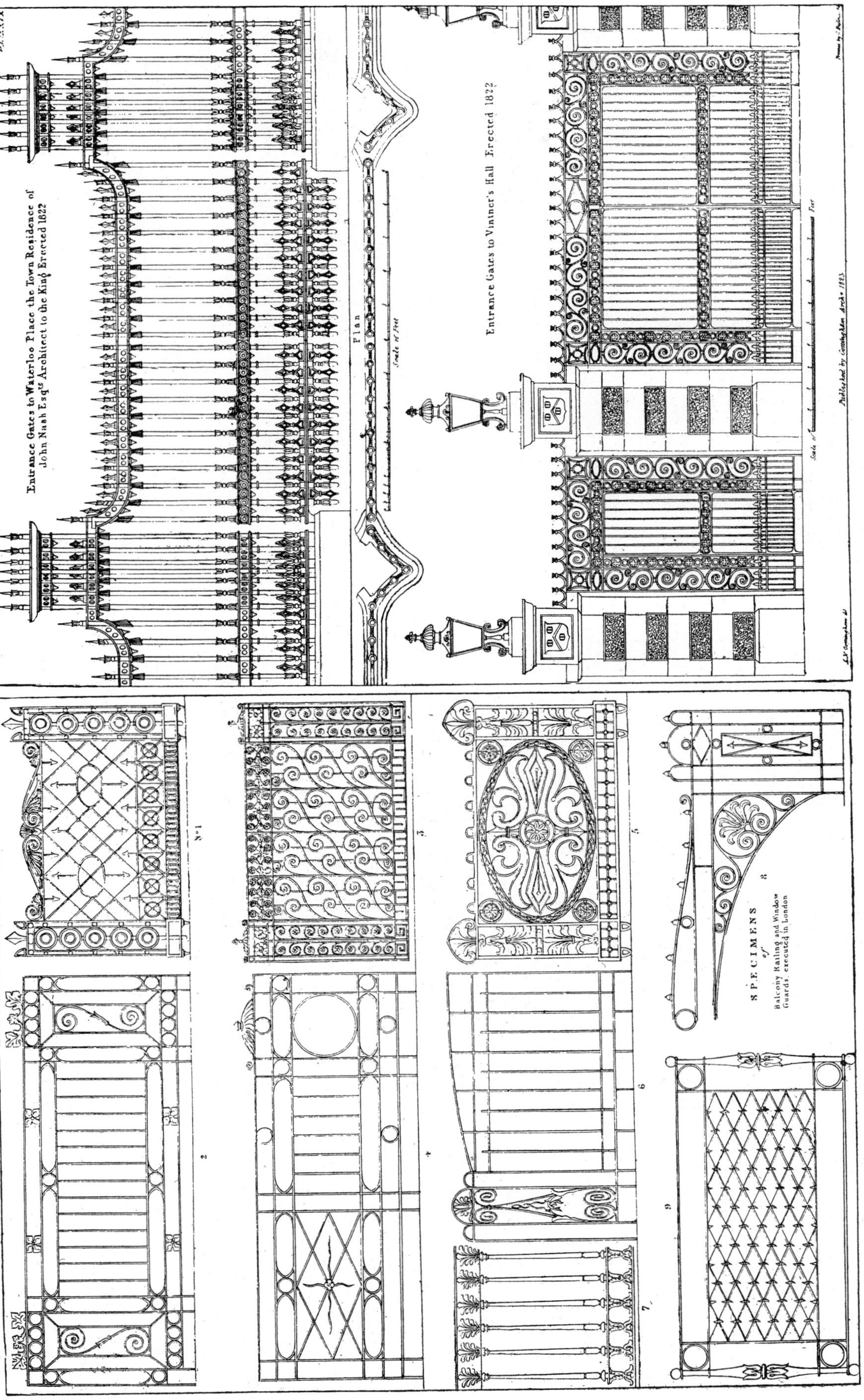

232.—PLATES FROM "THE SMITH AND FOUNDERS DIRECTOR," 1823.

(*By Cottingham, Architect.*)

233.—NORWICH GATES, SANDRINGHAM HOUSE, NORFOLK. A FINE EXAMPLE OF NINETEENTH CENTURY WROUGHT IRONWORK.

234.—GATES AT WEST END OF LAW COURTS, LONDON, BY STREET.

work its charm—that of the hand incapable of machine-like accuracy. It is a travesty that this should have happened just at the opening of the most prolific period of invention in machinery of every description. What could be more ludicrous than that, for many years past, it has been derogatory to style an article as " machine-made " ?

The re-birth of wrought iron as an art or craft may be placed at 1851, when the gates now standing at Sandringham were shown, and generally regarded as one of the finest exhibits of that year's Great Exhibition.

A little later that band of great men—Gardner, Phillips. Webb, Eden Nesfield, Morris, Burne-Jones, Norman Shaw and others—gradually began to get together workmen whom they taught to forget what they knew and learn the art of the picturesque.

235.—WALL SCONCE IN WROUGHT IRON, BY EDGAR BRANDT.

236.—" DIANA AND THE DEER." GRILLE IN WROUGHT IRON AND BRONZE, BY EDGAR BRANDT.

The travesty again appears in that it was not long before the ingenuity of the inventor's brain was busy creating machinery to produce articles with the definite and one intention of their appearing to have been made by hand.

During the last thirty years every means, fair and foul, has been used to recapture this old-world atmosphere of hand labour. Builders employed mostly in more costly domestic work have staffs of workmen who understand and appreciate what is required of them ; but it is still very common to find those who regard it as the act of a madman deliberately to use bent timbers, glass-paper down sharp, clean arrises, or call for rough, uneven surfaces.

237.—SCREEN IN HAMMERED IRON, BY EDGAR BRANDT.

238.—GATES IN WROUGHT IRON, BY EDGAR BRANDT.

A pitch of perfection, has, for some years, been arrived at in this copying of old work, and, while pure faking is to be deprecated, it is good that the due appreciation of texture and material has been revived.

This fashion for the sweetly pretty and obviously picturesque, together with the intensely dull, uninteresting academic work of the years previous to the war, made the younger and more adventurous spirits ready to break away. Aided by the turmoil and realism of the war, the ranks grew of those who were ready to accept anything unusual as being of great worth. Damned and derided by all the more established minds, the modern movement grew instead of withering, and has long since proved that its effort was not to be put aside and trampled upon as the output of degenerates.

The last few years have shown a remarkable advance in the taste of the public. Efficiency and consequent simplicity are appreciated to a greater extent, and this has, naturally, led to the lessening of meretricious ornament and the misuse of material. There is much honest seeking after not only new uses for materials, but new methods of use, together with a whole-hearted acceptance of machinery and all it can give.

All the crafts have shown a marked revival since the war, though the metal-working crafts are not so nimble as some others in following up fresh paths. In spite of the very remarkable achievements of Edgar Brandt and other French metal workers, very few English smiths have followed this lead, except in the case of designs for such minor works as hanging and wall-lamp fittings, in which the influence of Brandt's vigour and force and daring originality may be traced.

It is true that among the modern school morbid tendencies exist, but it would be truer to say that modern art and craftsmanship tend to escape the morbid features so prevalent since the war and to capture a spirit which is new, and yet old as Adam.

239.—MODERN HAMMERED WROUGHT-IRON GATES, MORTUARY CHAPEL, STOCKHOLM. DESIGNED BY GUNNAR ASPLUND, EXECUTED BY PETER ANDERSSEN OF MYRA.

(*Reproduced by permission of Messrs. Ernst B. Westman, Ltd.*)

BIBLIOGRAPHY

PAGE

An Account of the Iron Works in the Forest of Dean, by Henry Powles – – – 49, 70, 71
Agricola – – – – – – – – – – – – – – – – 8
Appraisement of the Goods and Chattels of Stephen le Northerne – – – – – – 23
Ashmole – – – – – – – – – – – – – – – – 41
Country Life – – – – – – – 64, 114, 127, 128, 139, 142, 147, 149, 151, 152, 153
Cygnus – – – – – – – – – – – – – – – – 64
Chronicles of the Collegiate Church of All Saints', Derby, by Dr. Charles Cox – – – 134, 135
Coming of the Steel. See *Rewards and Fairies.*
Decorative Ironwork from the Eleventh to the Eighteenth Century, by Mr. Charles ffoulkes – 18, 21, 30
Domestic Architecture in England – – – – – – – – – – – – – – 17
Eighteenth Century Architecture of Bristol, by Mr. Dening – – – – – – 121, 123, 124
England's Improvements by Sea and Land to Out-do the Dutch without Fighting, to Pay Debts without Moneys, by Andrew Yarranton, Gent., London – – – – – 49, 72
English Homes, by Mr. H. Avray Tipping, M.A., F.S.A. – – – – – – – – – – 139
English Industries of the Middle Ages, by L. F. Salzman, M.A., F.S.A. – – – – – – 8–12
English Ironwork of the Seventeenth and Eighteenth Centuries, by Mr. Starkie Gardner – – – – – – 56, 68, 101, 104, 107, 116, 139, 144, 151, 152, 158, 159, 172
Greater London, by Walford – – – – – – – – – – – – – – 172
Ironwork from the Earliest Times to the End of the Mediæval Period, by Mr. Starkie Gardner – – – – – – – – – – – – – – – 19, 28, 29, 42
Iron in Antiquity, by Friend – – – – – – – – – – – – – – 4
Manners and Household Expenses, Thirteenth and Fifteenth Centuries—Roxburghe Club – 21
Master Masons to the Crown of Scotland, by Mylne – – – – – – – – – – 56
Masterpieces of Industrial Art, International Exhibition, 1862, by Mr. J. B. Waring – 44
Memorials of London and London Life, Thirteenth, Fourteenth and Fifteenth Centuries, by Mr. H. T. Riley – – – – – – – – – – – – – – – 23
Metallurgy, by Percy – – – – – – – – – – – – – – 1, 2, 4, 13, 14
Metalwork, by Sir Matthew Wyatt – – – – – – – – – – – – – 25, 26
Natural History, by Pliny – – – – – – – – – – – – – – – 3
Ordinances of the Blacksmiths, Richard II – – – – – – – – – – – 16
Oxford, 1723–33, by Williams – – – – – – – – – – – – – – 172
Rewards and Fairies, by Rudyard Kipling – – – – – – – – – – – – 6
Royal Society's Philosophical Transactions, 1677–78. See *An Account of the Iron Works in the Forest of Dean.*
Sandford – – – – – – – – – – – – – – – – – 41
Some Account of the Worshipful Company of Ironworkers, by Mr. John Nicholls – 70
Sussex Archæological Society's "Transactions" – – – – – – – – – – – 44
Westminster Abbey, by G. G. Scott and others (Mr. Burgess) – – – – – – – 26, 27, 31
Westminster Abbey and Craftsmen, by Lethaby – – – – – – – – – – 21, 31
Westminster Abbey, by Francis Bond – – – – – – – – – – – – 16
Willsment, Mr. – – – – – – – – – – – – – – – – 38
Windsor Castle, by Sir St. John Hope – – – – – – – – 14, 15, 21, 34, 35, 37, 38, 41

INDEX

NOTE.—*The large numerals indicate* ILLUSTRATIONS *of the subject mentioned, and refer not to the figure numbers but to the pages on which illustrations will be found. The small numerals indicate* REFERENCES IN THE TEXT

ERRATA.

Page 35, line 10, "Figs. 45 and 46" should read "Figs. 44, 45 and 46."
Page 41, Fig. 53, "Swarford Church" should read "Snarford Church."
Page 57, line 7, "Fig. 67" should read "Fig. 66."
Page 67, line 39, "Monument" should read "Monmouthshire."